CULTURAL HERITAGE AND CONTEMPORARY CHANGE
SERIES I, CULTURE AND VALUES, VOLUME 21
SERIES IIA, ISLAM, VOLUME 12
General Editor
George F. McLean

RELIGION
and
COOPERATION
between
CIVILIZATIONS

Islamic and Christian Cultures
in a Global Horizon

GEORGE F. McLEAN

THE COUNCIL FOR RESEARCH IN VALUES AND PHILOSOPHY

Copyright © 2000 by
The Council for Research in Values and Philosophy

Box 261
Cardinal Station
Washington, D.C. 20064

Printed in the United States of America

Library of Congress Cataloging-in-Publication

McLean, George F.
Religion and cooperation between civilizations: Islamic and Christian cultures in a global horizon / George F. McLean.
    p. cm. — (Cultural heritage and contemporary change. Series I, culture and values, volume 21; Series IIA, Islam; vol. 12)
    Includes bibliographical references and index.
    1. Christianity and culture. 2. Islamic countries--Civilization. 3. Christianity and other religions--Islam. 4. Islam--Relations--Christianity.   I. Title.   II. Series.   III. Series: Cultural heritage and contemporary change. Series I, culture and values, volume 21; Series IIA, Islam; vol. 12
BR115.C8 2000
291.1'7—dc21   00-031603
                                                                              CIP

ISBN 1-56518-152-2 (paper)

CONTENTS

INTRODUCTION

The end of the 20th century marked the conclusion of the period of totalitarian ideologies. Finally the dehumanizing technological universalism which had so terrorized the world from the 1930s, through World War II and into the 1980s was displaced by a new awareness of the person and of human subjectivity. In the euphoria of 1989 the way appeared to open to a new utopia in which the creative freedom of peoples could be asserted, their values and virtues affirmed and their cultural traditions renewed.

Unfortunately — or more interestingly — life has not proven to be so simple. With the new recognition and even celebration of the cultural specificity of the many peoples has come competition, even conflict, sliding at times into genocide. Consequently, among the challenges which we face as we move into the 21st century perhaps the greatest is to find the resources and the creativity to be able to live these cultures fully in a way that can generate not conflict, but cooperation between them.

At base this is an issue of whether reality as such — and in particular human reality — is to be comprehended in terms of matter, colliding atoms and nuclear conflict or in terms of the spirit and hence bonds of sharing and love. Indeed, even when Samuel Huntington rooted civilizations in religion, he still interpreted them according to former models as basically conflictual.

It is necessary then to study in depth the nature of cultural traditions as human artifacts and especially the interpretation of their mutual relations. This has been the subject of a number of studies and conferences, especially in Islamic contexts. There the special concern to be faithful to the message of the Prophet received in the past makes particularly important the hermeneutic issue of how this can be read in a way that ground and enables the onward progress of life in new times.

Hence Part I is entitled "Hermeneutics as the Interpretation and Interchange of Cultures". Chapter I, "Hermeneutics of Cultural Traditions and Their Religious Roots" concerns directly the hermeneutic issue of cultures in order to look intensively into their constitution and interpretation. It traces this issue to the religious roots of cultures and civilizations.

Chapter II, "Cultural Traditions as Prospective and Progressive (Tashkent Lecture, 1999)" was written in response to the question of whether tradition is a block to progress. This has been claimed by classical liberalism which emphasizes "freedom from" in order to be unlimited in one's choice. This lecture given at the philosophy summer school in Tashkent in 1999 looks at tradition in its diachronic and prospective character as a progressive force.

Chapter III, "Hermeneutics and Cultures (Tehran Lecture, 1999)," given at the Mulla Sadra conference in Tehran in 1999 reviews some of the same matters with special attention to the implications of hermeneutics for cultural studies.

Part II is entitled "Globalization as Relations between Cultures". Here Chapter IV, "Nicholas of Cusa: an Epistemology and Metaphysics for Globalization as Diversity in Unity (Conference on the Philosophical Challenges and Opportunities of Globalization, Boston, 1998)" is concerned to resituate the issue of the relation between cultures in the new global context. But to do so requires a new epistemology and metaphysics. This will take considerable time to develop, but it promises to be a major challenge and contribution of the third millennium.

However, it is possible to reach into the treasure house of earlier work in philosophy to find at the break between Medieval and Renaissance thought the sketch of a new way of thinking achieved by one who has been called the last of the medievals and the first of the Renaissance minds, namely, Nicholas of Cusa. His sense of the human, precisely in contrast to the divine, was that because it was limited it needed multiplicity and diversity, that is, it needed the whole of creation in order to reflect the infinite and All-Perfect which is as well the One act of creative love. From this it follows that each is a contraction of the whole and related inherently to all else. This provides the basis for a new way of thinking that is truly global in character. This paper was prepared initially for the joint meeting of the International Society for Metaphysics (ISM), the World Union of Catholic Philosophical Societies (WUCPS) and the Council for Research in Values and Philosophy (RVP) on "Philosophical Challenges and Opportunities of Globalization" in Boston in 1998 on the occasion of the 20th World Congress of Philosophy.

Part III "Religion and Cooperation between Peoples and Cultures" deepens the discussion of the role of religion in the dialogue between cultures. If the source and goal of being is God and if cultures are the patterns of human understanding and commitment, then religion as the relation of humans, persons and societies to God must be the basis for cultures. In this light, issues of relations between cultures are rooted in relations between religions. Hence this part begins with Chapter V, "Cultures, Religions and Relations between Peoples," to lay the foundations for the investigation of whether this relationship of cultures and more radically of religions is in principle one of harmony or of conflict. As with Chapter I, this provides more detail for the chapters which follow in this Part.

Chapter VI, "The Relation of Islamic and Christian Cultures," treats a special instance, namely, the relation between Islamic and Christian cultures. After long defining themselves in contrast one to the other, the two are now embarked on a project of mutual positive discovery. The need for this is only intensified by the processes of modernization and of East-West interaction in a global world of economics, communication and culture. This lecture was delivered at the conference in Bulgaria in 1998 on "Islamic and Christian Dialogue".

Chapter VII, "Islam as Seen from the Christian West (Al-Azhar, 1994)," goes more deeply into the way in which Islam and Christianity see each other. Great progress has taken place on this in recent years, led by the al-Azhar University in Cairo, which was the site of this lecture in 1994.

But this issue is not only one of cultures, but of mega-units or whole civilizations. It extends from relations between cultures to relations between civilizations. Here a key work has been that of Samuel Huntington, *The Clash of Civilization and the Remaking of World Order*. His thesis, as noted above, is that the identities of the several civilizations are rooted in religion and that all identities are conflictual.

This thesis is developed in Chapter VIII, "Samuel Huntington and the Religious Basis for Civilization," a lecture presented in Tehran in 1998 at the Center for Cultural Research. It is redeveloped and subjected to critique in Chapter IX, "Conflict or Cooperation between Civilizations," delivered at the Institute for Dialogue between Civilizations in Tehran in 1999. The Chapter draws upon a number of the earlier chapters to develop, in contrast to Huntington, the conditions not for conflict, but for dialogue and cooperation between civilization. This is based on their religious character as calling for a transcendence of egoism in favor of cooperation between peoples on a shared pilgrimage from different quadrants, but toward the one Holy Mountain (Isaiah 27:13).

George F. McLean

PART I

HERMENEUTICS AS
THE INTERPRETATION AND
INTERCHANGE OF CULTURES

CHAPTER I

HERMENEUTICS OF CULTURAL TRADITIONS AND THEIR RELIGIOUS ROOTS

The emerging appreciation of subjectivity has brought new appreciation of the being and hence the life of human being. As such it is the concrete exercise of freedom which is lived in a cultural tradition and in the structures of civil society. This chapter unfolds the import of this appreciation. It will concern first freedom as the properly human exercise of life and being, and second the pattern of values and virtues as this constitutes the cultural tradition which shapes that freedom as lived by a people. Our concern will be to understand this deeply as constituting the religious. Hence we shall constitute the pilgrimage of peoples. In what sense is this a way to God?

To examine this in detail the present chapter will begin with an analysis of levels of the freedom. It will relate them to the structure of the critiques of Kant in order to follow the epistemology each entails and to open the way to freedom as the human exercise of existence, the metaphysical center of human life. Second, on this basis it will turn to the constitution of a culture not as an empirical object of anthropological codification, but as the corporate exercise of the freedom of a people. Third, in order to engage this issue existentially, the chapter will then turn to civil society as the new emergence of freedom in these post-totalitarian times considering the reconstruction of social life as religious action, and finally to an issue this entails, namely, democracy in a situation of religious pluralism.

This brings us to the challenge of our times, namely, whether a people can truly govern itself through the exercise of freedom. That is, can the cultural traditions of a people which are constituted of its cumulative freedom and religiously grounded hold sufficient authority or directive power to bring together a diversified civil society in its own governance. This is, in a way, a translation of Kant's requirement of autonomy rather than heteronomy, but here the autonomy being sought is not that of a secular rebellion against

God or of an individual only, but the proper autonomy to the human person as a creature of God and member of society.

LEVELS OF INSIGHT AND LEVELS OF FREEDOM

If freedom is the responsible exercise of our life then it can be understood how the search for freedom is central to our lives as persons and peoples. But the term is used so broadly and with so many meanings that it can both lead and mislead. It seems important then to sort out the various meanings of freedom.

After surveying carefully the history of ideas, Mortimer Adler and his team, in *The Idea of Freedom: A Dialectic Examination of the Conceptions of Freedom* (Garden City: Doubleday, 1958), outlined three levels of freedom: circumstantial freedom of self-realization as a choice of whatever I want among objects; acquired freedom of self-perfection as the ability to choose as we ought; and natural freedom of self-determination by which we responsibly create ourselves and our world.

Empirical Freedom of Choice

At the beginning of the modern stirrings for democracy John Locke perceived a crucial condition for a liberal democracy. If decisions were to be made not by the king but by the people, the basis for these decisions had to be equally available to all. To achieve this Locke proposed that we suppose the mind to be a blank paper void of characters and ideas, and then follow the way in which it comes to be furnished. To keep this public he insisted that it be done exclusively via experience, that is, either by sensation or by reflection upon the mind's work on the materials derived from the senses.[1] Proceeding on these suppositions as if they were real limitations of knowledge, David Hume concluded that all objects of knowledge which are not formal tautologies must be matters of fact. Such "matters of fact" are neither the existence nor the actuality of a thing nor its essence, but simply the determination of one from a pair of sensible contraries, e.g., white rather than black, sweet rather than sour.[2]

The restrictions implicit in this appear starkly in Rudolf Carnap's "Vienna Manifesto" which shrinks the scope of meaningful knowledge and significant discourse to describing "some state of affairs" in terms of empirical "sets of facts." This excludes speech about wholes, God, the unconscious or *entelechies*; the grounds of meaning, indeed all that transcends the immediate content of sense experience are excluded.[3]

The socio-political structures which have emerged from this model of Locke have contributed much, but a number of indices suggest that he and others have tried too hard to work out their model on a solely empirical or forensic basis. For in such terms it is not possible to speak of appropriate or inappropriate goals or even to evaluate choices in relation to self-fulfillment. The only concern is the ability to choose among a set of contraries by brute, changeable and even arbitrary will power, and whether circumstances will allow me to carry out that choice. Such choices, of course, may not only differ from, but even contradict the immediate and long range objectives of other persons. This will require compromises in the sense of Hobbes; John Rawls will even work out a formal set of such compromises.[4]

Through it all, however, the basic concern remains the ability to do as one pleases: "being able to act or not act, according as we shall choose or will".[5] Its orientation is external. In practice as regards oneself, over time this comes to constitute a black hole of [self-centered] consumption of physical goods in which both nature and the person are consumed. This is the essence of consumerism; it shrinks the very notion of freedom to competitiveness in the pursuit of material wealth.

Freedom in this sense remains basically Hobbes's principle of conflict; it is the liberal ideology built upon the conception of human nature as corrupted, of man as wolf, and of life as conflict. Hopefully this will be exercised in an "enlightened" manner, but in this total inversion of human meaning and dignity laws and rights can be only external remedies. By doing violence to man's naturally violent tendencies, they attempt to attenuate to the minimal degree necessary one's free and self-centered choices and hence the supposed basic viciousness of human life. There must be better understandings of human freedom and indeed these emerge as soon as one looks beyond external objects to the interior nature and the existence of the human subject and of all reality.

Formal Freedom to Choose as One Ought

For Kant the heteronomous, external and empiricist character of the above disqualifies it from being moral at all, much less
from constituting human freedom. In his first *Critique of Pure
Reason* Kant had studied the role of the mind in the scientific
constitution of the universe. He reasoned that because our sense
experience was always limited and partial, the universality and
necessity of the laws of science must come from the human mind.
This was an essential turning point for it directed attention to the
role of the human spirit and especially to the reproductive imagination in constituting the universe in which we live and move.

But this is not the realm of freedom, for if the forms and
categories with which we work are from our mind, how we construct
with them is not left to our discretion. The imagination must bring
together the multiple elements of sense intuition in a unity or order
capable of being informed by the concepts or categories of the
intellect with a view to constituting the necessary and universal
judgments of science. The subject's imagination here is active but
not free, for it is ruled by the categories integral to the necessary
and universal judgements of the sciences. In these terms the human
mind remains merely an instrument of physical progress and a
function of matter.

However, in his second *Critique*, that of *Practical Reason*,
beyond the set of universal, necessary and ultimately material
relations, Kant points to the reality of human responsibility. This is
the reality of freedom or spirit which characterizes and distinguishes the person. In its terms he recasts the whole notion of physical
law as moral rule. If freedom is not to be chaotic and randomly
destructive, it must be ruled or under law. To be free is to be able to
will as I ought, i.e., in conformity with moral law.

Yet in order to be free the moral act must be autonomous.
Hence, my maxim must be something which as a moral agent I —
and no other —give to myself. Finally, though I am free because I
am the lawmaker, my exercise of this power cannot be arbitrary if
the moral order must be universal.

On this basis, a new level of freedom emerges. It is not merely
self-centered whimsy in response to circumstantial stimuli; nor is it
a despotic exercise of power or the work of the clever self-serving

eye of Plato's rogue. Rather, it is the highest reality in all creation. To will as I ought is wise and caring power, open to all and bent upon the realization of "the glorious ideal of a universal realm of ends-in-themselves". In sum, it is free men living together in righteous harmony. This is what we are really about; it is our glory — and our burden.

Unfortunately, for Kant this glorious ideal remained on the formal plane; it was a matter of essence rather than of existence. It was intended as a guiding principle, a critical norm to evaluate the success or failure of the human endeavor — but it was not the human endeavor itself. For failure to appreciate this, much work for human rights remains at a level of abstraction which provides only minimal requirements. It might found processes of legal redress, but stops short of — and may even distract from and thus impede — positive engagement in the real process of constructing the world in which we live: witness the long paralysis of Europe and the world in the face of the Jugoslav dissolution of the moral and hence legal foundations of Europe.

This second level of freedom makes an essential contribution to human life; we must not forget it nor must we ever do less. But it does not give us the way in which we as unique people in this unique time and space face our concrete problems. We need common guides, but our challenge is to act concretely. Can philosophy, without becoming politics or other processes of social action, consider and contribute to the actual process of human existence as we shape and implement our lives in freedom?

When the contemporary mind proceeds beyond objective and formal natures to become more deeply conscious of human subjectivity, and of existence precisely as emerging from and through human self-awareness, then the most profound changes must take place. The old order built on objective structures and norms would no longer be adequate; structures would crumble and a new era would dawn. This is indeed the juncture at which we now stand.

Existential Freedom of Self-determination and Self-Constitution

Progress in being human corresponds to the deepening of one's sense of being, beyond Platonic forms and structures, essences and laws, to act as uncovered by Aristotle and especially to existence as it emerges in Christian philosophy through the Patristic and Middle Ages. More recently this sensibility to existence has emerged anew through the employment of a phenomenological method for focusing upon intentionality and the self-awareness of the human person in time (*dasein*). This opens to the third level of freedom stated above, namely, that of deciding for oneself in virtue of the power "inherent in human nature to change one's own character creatively and to determine what one shall be or shall become." This is the most radical freedom, namely, our natural freedom of self-determination.

This basically is self-affirmation in terms of our teleological orientation toward perfection or full realization, which we will see to be the very root of the development of values, of virtues and hence of cultural traditions. It implies seeking perfection when it is absent and enjoying or celebrating it when attained. In this sense, it is that stability in one's orientation to the good which classically has been termed holiness and anchors such great traditions of the world as the Hindu and Taoist, Islamic and the Judeo-Christian. One might say that this is life as practiced archetypically by the saints and holy men, but it would be more correct to say that it is because they lived in such a manner that they are called holy.

In his third *Critique,* Kant suggests an important insight regarding how this might form a creative force for confronting present problems and hence for passing on the tradition in a transforming manner. He sees that if the free person of the second Critique were to be surrounded by the necessitarian universe of the first Critique, then one's freedom would be entrapped and entombed within one's mind, while one's external actions would be necessary and necessitated. If there is to be room for human freedom in a cosmos in which one can make use of necessary laws, indeed if science is to contribute to the exercise of human freedom, then nature too must be understood as directed toward a goal and must manifest throughout a teleology within which free human purpose can be integrated. In these terms, even in its necessary and universal laws, nature is no longer alien to freedom; rather it expresses divine freedom and is conciliable with human freedom.

This makes possible the exercise of freedom, but our issue is how this freedom is exercised in a way that creates diverse cultures as ways to God, i.e., how can a free person relate to an order of nature and to structures of society in a way that is neither neces sitated nor necessitating, but free and creative? In the "Critique of the Aesthetic Judgment," Kant points out that in working toward an integrating unity the imagination is not confined by the necessitating structures of categories and concepts as in the first *Critique*, or the regulating ideal of the second *Critique*. Returning to the order of essences would lose the uniqueness of the self and its freedom. Rather, the imagination ranges freely over the full sweep of reality in all its dimensions to see where relatedness and purposiveness can emerge. This ordering and reordering by the imagination can bring about numberless unities or patterns of actions and natures. Unrestricted by any *a priori* categories, it can integrate necessary dialectical patterns within its own free and creative productions and include scientific universals within its unique concrete harmonies. This is the proper and creative work of the human person in this world.

In order for human freedom to be sensitive to the entirety of this all-encompassing harmony, in the final analysis our conscious attention must be directed not merely to universal and necessary physical or social structures, nor even to beauty and ugliness either in their concrete empirical realizations or in their Platonic ideals. Rather, our focus must be upon the integrating images of pleasure or displeasure, enjoyment or revulsion, generated deep within our person by these images as we attempt to shape our world according to the relation of our will to the good and hence to realize the good for our times.

In fact, however, this is still a matter of forms and categories, rather than of existence. Further it is a matter of the human person in him- or herself. But it is possible in the light of the progress in philosophy and specifically on existence made at the time of the early Church Fathers to read this work in terms of existence in relation to creation rather than of essence. The aesthetic enables one to follow the free exercise of existence in a human life. At this point then the third level of freedom becomes truly the work of God with us.

In this manner human freedom becomes at once the goal, the creative source, the manifestation, the evaluation and the arbiter of all that imaginatively we can propose. It is *goal*, namely to realize life as rational and free in this world; it is *creative source*, for through the imagination freedom unfolds the endless possibilities for human expression; it is *manifestation* because it presents these to our consciousness in ways appropriate to our capabilities for knowledge of limited realities and relates these to the circumstances of our life; it is *criterion* because its response manifests a possible mode of action to be variously desirable or not in terms of a total personal response of pleasure or displeasure, enjoyment or revulsion; and it is *arbiter* because it provides the basis upon which our freedom chooses to affirm or reject, realize or avoid this mode of self-realization.

Thus, freedom in this third, existential sense emerges as the dynamic center of our life. It is the spectroscope and kaleidoscope through which is processed the basic thrust toward perfection upon which, as we shall see, culture as the pattern of public life is based and by which its orders of preference or values are set. The philosophical and religious traditions it creates become the keys to the dynamics of human life. Hence the possibilities of peace within a nation and cooperation between peoples must depend fundamentally on the potentialities of creative freedom for overcoming the proclivities of the first level of freedom for confrontation and violent competition, for surmounting the general criteria of the second level of freedom, and for setting in motion positive processes of concrete peaceful and harmonious collaboration.

CULTURAL TRADITION AS CUMULATIVE FREEDOM SHAPING A PATTERN FOR LIFE: THE SYNCHRONIC DIMENSION

It is not sufficient, however, to consider only the freedom of single actors for that could leave a human, and *a fortiori* a social life, chaotic and inconsistent. Hence, it is necessary to see how the exercise of freedom is oriented and enabled over time by persons and peoples.

Value

The drama of this free self-determination, and hence the development of persons and of civil society, is a most fundamental matter, namely, that of being as affirmation or as definitive stance against non-being. The account of this and its implication was the work of Parmenides, the very first metaphysician. Identically this is the relation to the good in search of which we live, survive and thrive. The good is manifest in experience as the object of desire, namely, as that which is sought when absent. Basically, it is what completes life; it is the "per-fect", understood in its etymological sense as that which is completed or realized through and through. Hence, once achieved, it is no longer desired or sought, but enjoyed. This is reflected in the manner in which each thing, even a stone, retains the being or reality it has and resists reduction to non-being or nothing. The most that we can do is to change or transform a thing into something else; we cannot annihilate it. Similarly, a plant or tree, given the right conditions, grows to full stature and fruition. Finally, an animal protects its life — fiercely, if necessary — and seeks out the food needed for its strength. Food, in turn, as capable of contributing to an animal's realization or perfection, is for the animal an auxiliary good or means.

In this manner, things as good, that is, as actually realizing some degree of perfection and able to contribute to the well-being of others, are the bases for an interlocking set of relations. As these relations are based upon both the actual perfection things possess and the potential perfection to which they are thereby directed, the good is perfection both as attracting when it has not yet been attained and as constituting one's fulfillment upon its achievement. Goods, then, are not arbitrary or simply a matter of wishful thinking; they are rather the full development of things and all that contributes thereto. In this ontological or objective sense, all beings are good to the extent that they exist and can contribute to the perfection of others.

The moral good is a more narrow field, for it concerns only one's free and responsible actions. This has the objective reality of the ontological good noted above, for it concerns real actions which stand in distinctive relation to our own perfection and to that of others — and, indeed, to the physical universe and to God as well. Hence, many possible patterns of actions could be objectively right because they promote the good of those involved, while others, precisely as inconsistent with the real good of persons or things, are objectively disordered or misordered. This constitutes the objective basis for the ethical good or bad.

Nevertheless, because the realm of objective relations is almost numberless, whereas our actions are single, it is necessary not only to choose in general between the good and the bad, but in each case to choose which of the often innumerable possibilities one will render concrete.

However broad or limited the options, as responsible and moral, an act is essentially dependent upon its being willed by a subject. Therefore, in order to follow the emergence of the field of concrete moral action, it is not sufficient to examine only the objective aspect, namely the nature of the things involved. In addition, one must consider the action in relation to the subject, namely, to the person who, in the context of his/her society and culture, appreciates and values the good of this action, chooses it over its alternatives, and eventually wills its actualization.

The term 'value' here is of special note. It was derived from the economic sphere where it meant the amount of a commodity sufficient to attain a certain worth. This is reflected also in the term 'axiology' whose root means "weighing as much" or "worth as much." It requires an objective content — the good must truly "weigh in" and make a real difference; but the term 'value' expresses this good especially as related to wills which actually acknowledge it as a good and as desirable.[6] Thus, different individuals or groups of persons and at different periods have distinct sets of values. A people or community is sensitive to, and prizes, a distinct set of goods or, more likely, it establishes a distinctive ranking in the degree to which it prizes various goods. By so doing, it delineates among limitless objective goods a certain pattern of values which in a more stable fashion mirrors the corporate free choices of that people.

This constitutes the basic topology of a culture; as repeatedly reaffirmed through time, it builds a tradition or heritage about which we shall speak below. It constitutes, as well, the prime pattern and gradation of goods or values which persons experience from their earliest years and in terms of which they interpret their developing relations. Young persons peer out at the world through lenses formed, as it were, by their family and culture and configured according to the pattern of choices made by that community throughout its history — often in its most trying circumstances. Like a pair of glasses it does not create the object; but it focuses attention upon certain goods involved rather than upon others. This becomes the basic orienting factor for the affective and emotional life described by the Scots, Adam Ferguson and Adam Smith, as the heart of civil society. In time, it encourages and reinforces certain patterns of action which, in turn, reinforce the pattern of values.

Through this process a group constitutes the concerns in terms of which it struggles to advance or at least to perdure, mourns its failures, and celebrates its successes. This is a person's or people's world of hopes and fears, in terms of which, as Plato wrote in the *Laches*, their lives have moral meaning.[7] It is varied according to the many concerns and the groups which coalesce around them. As these are interlocking and interdependent a pattern of social goals and concerns develops which guides action. In turn, corresponding capacities for action or virtue are developed.

Aristotle takes this up at the very beginning of his ethics. In order to make sense of the practical dimension of our life it is necessary to identify the good or value toward which one directs one's life or which one finds satisfying. This he terms happiness and then proceeds systematically to see which goal can be truly satisfying. His test is not passed by physical goods or honors, but by that which corresponds to, and fulfills, our highest capacity, that is, contemplation of the highest being or divine life.[8]

But what is the relation of this approach from below, as it were, to religion as seen from above, that is, from the point of view of revelation and grace which point to a more perfect goal and fulfillment? Thomas Aquinas's effort in his *Summa contra Gentiles*, analyzed by G. Stanley,[9] is to show the way in which this latter sense of religion is not a contradiction or substitution of the former, but rather its more perfect fulfillment than is possible by human powers alone. In eschatology the vision of God is not a negation of the contemplation of divine life of which Aristotle spoke, but its fulfillment in a way that exceeds human hopes.

Virtues

Martin Heidegger describes a process by which the self emerges as a person in the field of moral action. It consists in transcending oneself or breaking beyond mere self-concern and projecting outward as a being whose very nature is to share with others for whom one cares and about whom one is concerned. In this process, one identifies new purposes or goals for the sake of which action is to be undertaken. In relation to these goals, certain combinations of possibilities, with their natures and norms, take on particular importance and begin thereby to enter into the makeup of one's world of meaning.[10] Freedom then becomes more than mere spontaneity, more than choice, and more even than self-determination in the sense of determining oneself to act as described above. It shapes — the phenomenologist would say even that it constitutes — one's world as the ambit of human decisions and dynamic action. This is the making of the complex social ordering of social groups which constitutes civil society.

This process of deliberate choice and decision transcends the somatic and psychic dynamisms. The somatic dimension is extensively reactive; the psychic dynamisms of affectivity or appetite are fundamentally oriented to the good and positively attracted by a set of values. These, in turn, evoke an active response from the emotions in the context of responsible freedom. But it is in the dimension of responsibility that one encounters the properly moral and social dimension of life. For, in order to live with others, one must be able to know, to choose and finally to realize what is truly conducive to one's good and to that of others. Thus, persons and groups must be able to judge the true value of what is to be chosen, that is, its objective worth, both in itself and in relation to others. This is moral truth: the judgment regarding whether the act makes the person and society good in the sense of bringing authentic individual and social fulfillment, or the contrary.

In this, deliberation and voluntary choice are required in order to exercise proper self-awareness and self-governance. By determining to follow this judgment one is able to overcome determination by stimuli and even by culturally ingrained values and to turn these, instead, into openings for free action in concert with others in order to shape my community as well as my physical surroundings. This can be for good or for ill, depending on the character of my actions. By definition, only morally good actions contribute to personal and social fulfillment, that is, to the development and perfection of persons with others in community.

It is the function of conscience, as one's moral judgment, to identify this character of moral good in action. Hence, moral freedom consists in the ability to follow one's conscience. This work of conscience is not a merely theoretical judgment, but the exercise of self-possession and self-determination in one's actions. Here, reference to moral truth constitutes one's sense of duty, for the action that is judged to be truly good is experienced also as that which I ought to do.

When this is exercised or lived, patterns of action develop which are habitual in the sense of being repeated. These are the modes of activity with which we are familiar; in their exercise, along with the coordinated natural dynamisms they require, we are practiced; and with practice comes facility and spontaneity. Such patterns constitute the basic, continuing and pervasive shaping influence of our life. For this reason, they have been considered classically to be the basic indicators of what our life as a whole will add up to, or, as is often said, "amount to". Since Socrates, the technical term for these especially developed capabilities has been `virtues' or special strengths.

But, if the ability to follow one's conscience and, hence, to develop one's set of virtues must be established through the interior dynamisms of the person, it must be protected and promoted by the related physical and social realities. This is a basic right of the person--perhaps *the* basic human and social right — because only thus can one transcend one's conditions and strive for fulfillment. Its protection and promotion must be a basic concern of any order which would be democratic and directed to the good of its people.

But this is only a right to one's conscience; religion goes further in that it looks to divine grace for help. Some virtues are the result not only of human practice, but of divine action. In other words the perspective shifts from the secondary causality of the human creature to the primary casualty of the divine existent itself. Its effect is created existence with its truth, justice and faith; love that expresses the goodness of the creator as source and goal; and ecstasy in response to the sublime beauty of the divine.

Cultural Tradition as Synchronic

Together, these values and virtues of a people set the pattern of social life through which freedom is developed and exercised. This is called a "culture". On the one hand, the term is derived from the Latin word for tilling or cultivating the land. Cicero and other Latin authors used it for the cultivation of the soul or mind (*cultura animi*), for just as even good land, when left without cultivation, will produce only disordered vegetation of little value, so the human spirit will not achieve its proper results unless trained or educated.[11] This sense of culture corresponds most closely to the Greek term for education (*paideia*) as the development of character, taste and judgment, and to the German term "formation" (*Bildung*).[12]

Here, the focus is upon the creative capacity of the spirit of a people and their ability to work as artists, not only in the restricted sense of producing purely aesthetic objects, but in the more involved sense of shaping all dimensions of life, material and spiritual, economic and political. The result is a whole life, characterized by unity and truth, goodness and beauty, and, thereby, sharing deeply in meaning and value. The capacity for this cannot be taught, although it may be enhanced by education; more recent phenomenological and hermeneutic inquiries suggest that, at its base, culture is a renewal, a reliving of origins in an attitude of profound appreciation.[13] This leads us beyond self and other, beyond identity and diversity, in order to comprehend both.

On the other hand, "culture" can be traced to the term *civis* (citizen, civil society and civilization).[14] This reflects the need for a person to belong to a social group or community in order for the human spirit to produce its proper results. By bringing to the person the resources of the tradition, the *tradita* or past wisdom produced by the human spirit, the community facilitates comprehension. By enriching the mind with examples of values which have been identified in the past, it teaches and inspires one to produce something analogous. For G.F. Klemm, this more objective sense of culture is composite in character.[15] E.B. Tyler defined this classically for the social sciences as "that complex whole which includes knowledge, belief, art, morals, law, customs and any other capabilities and habits required by man as a member of society."[16]

In contrast, Clifford Geertz came to focus on the meaning of all this for a people and on how a people's intentional action went about shaping its world. Thus he contrasts the analysis of culture to an experimental science in search of laws, seeing it rather as an interpretative science in search of meaning.[17] What is sought is the import of artifacts and actions, that is, whether "it is, ridicule or challenge, irony or anger, snobbery or pride, that, in their occurrence and through their agency, is getting said."[18] For this there is need to be aware "of the imaginative universe within which their acts are signs."[19] In this light, Geertz defines culture rather as "an historically transmitted pattern of meanings embodied in symbols, a system of intended conceptions expressed in symbolic forms by means of which men communicate, perpetuate and develop their knowledge about and attitudes toward life."[20]

Each particular complex whole or culture is specific to a particular people; a person who shares in this is a *civis* or citizen and belongs to a civilization. For the more restricted Greek world in which this term was developed, others (aliens) were those who did not speak the Greek tongue; they were "barbaroi", for their speech sounded like mere babel. Though at first this meant simply non-Greek, its negative manner of expression easily lent itself to, perhaps reflected, and certainly favored, a negative axiological connotation; indeed, this soon became the primary meaning of the word `barbarian'. By reverse implication, it attached to the term `civilization' an exclusivist connotation, such that the cultural identity of peoples began to imply not only the pattern of gracious symbols by which one encounters and engages in shared life projects with other persons and peoples, but cultural alienation between peoples. Today, as communication increases and more widely differentiated peoples enter into ever greater interaction and mutual dependence, we reap a bitter harvest of this negative connotation. The development of a less exclusivist sense of culture and civilization must be a priority task.

The development of values and virtues and their integration as a culture of any depth or richness takes time, and hence depends upon the experience and creativity of many generations. Taken as cultural inheritance, it reflects the cumulative achievement of a people in discovering, mirroring and transmitting the deepest meanings of life. This is tradition in its synchronic sense as a body of wisdom.

This sense of tradition is very vivid in premodern and village communities. It would appear to be much less so in modern urban centers, undoubtedly in part due to the difficulty in forming active community life in large urban centers. However, the cumulative process of transmitting, adjusting and applying the values of a culture through time is not only heritage or what is received, but new creation as this is passed on in new ways. Attending to tradition, taken in this active sense, allows us not only to uncover the permanent and universal truths which Socrates sought, but to perceive the importance of values we receive from the tradition and to mobilize our own life projects actively toward the future. We will look at this more active sense of tradition as diachronic below.

The Genesis of Culture in Community

Because tradition has sometimes been interpreted as a threat to the personal and social freedom essential to a democracy, it is important to see how a cultural tradition is generated by the free and responsible life of the members of a concerned community or civil society and enables succeeding generations to realize their life with freedom and creativity. This will be considered with special attention to ways to God and to religious traditions as lived in religious communities and their role in enlivening and supporting persons and groups on their way to God.

Autogenesis is no more characteristic of the birth of knowledge than it is of persons. One's consciousness emerges, not with self, but in relation to others. In the womb, the first awareness is that of the heart beat of one's mother. Upon birth, one enters a family in whose familiar relations one is at peace and able to grow. It is from one's family and in one's earliest weeks and months that one does or does not develop the basic attitudes of trust and confidence which undergird or undermine one's capacities for subsequent social relations. There one encounters care and concern for others independently of what they do for us and acquires the language and symbol system in terms of which to conceptualize, communicate and understand.[21] Just as a person is born into a family on which he or she depends absolutely for life, sustenance, protection and promotion, so one's understanding develops in community. As persons we emerge by birth into a family and neighborhood from which we learn and in harmony with which we may thrive.

Similarly, through the various steps of one's development, as one's circle of community expands through neighborhood, school, work and recreation, one comes to learn and to share personally and passionately an interpretation of reality and a pattern of value responses. The phenomenologist sees this life in the varied civil society as the new source for wisdom. Hence, rather than turning away from daily life in order to contemplate abstract and disembodied ideas, the place to discover meaning is in life as lived in the family and in the progressively wider social circles into which one enters.

If it were merely a matter of community, however, all might be limited to the present, with no place for tradition as that which is "passed on" from one generation to the next. In fact, the process of trial and error, of continual correction and addition in relation to a people's evolving sense of human dignity and purpose, constitutes a type of learning and testing laboratory for successive generations. In this laboratory of history, the strengths of various insights and behavior patterns can be identified and reinforced, while deficiencies are progressively corrected or eliminated. Horizontally, we learn from experience what promotes and what destroys life and, accordingly, make pragmatic adjustments.

But even this language remains too abstract, too limited to method or technique, too unidimensional. While tradition can be described in general and at a distance in terms of feedback mechanisms and might seem merely to concern how to cope in daily life, what is being spoken about are free acts that are expressive of passionate human commitment and personal sacrifice in responding to concrete danger, building and rebuilding family alliances and constructing and defending one's nation. Moreover, this wisdom is not a matter of mere tactical adjustments to temporary concerns; it concerns rather the meaning we are able to envision for life and which we desire to achieve through all such adjustments over period of generations, i.e., what is truly worth striving for and the pattern of social interaction in which this can be lived richly. The result of this extended process of learning and commitment constitutes our awareness of the bases for the decisions of which history is constituted.

This points us beyond the horizontal plane of the various ages of history and directs our attention vertically to its ground and, hence, to the bases of the values which humankind in its varied circumstances seeks to realize.[22] It is here that one searches for the absolute ground of meaning and value of which Iqbal wrote. Without that all is ultimately relative to only an interlocking network of consumption, then dissatisfaction and finally ennui.

The impact of the convergence of cumulative experience and reflection is heightened by its gradual elaboration in ritual and music, and its imaginative configuration in such great epics as the *Mahabharata* and in dance. All conspire to constitute a culture which, like a giant telecommunications dish, shapes, intensifies and extends the range and penetration of our personal sensitivity, free decision and mutual concern.

Tradition, then, is not, as in history, simply everything that ever happened, whether good or bad. It is rather what appears significant for human life: it is what has been seen through time and human experience to be deeply true and necessary for human life. It contains the values to which our forebears first freely gave their passionate commitment in specific historical circumstances and then constantly reviewed, rectified and progressively passed on generation after generation. The content of a tradition, expressed in works of literature and all the many facets of a culture, emerges progressively as something upon which character and community can be built. It constitutes a rich source from which multiple themes can be drawn, provided it be accepted and embraced, affirmed and cultivated.

Hence, it is not because of personal inertia on our part or arbitrary will on the part of our forbears that our culture provides a model and exemplar. On the contrary, the importance of tradition derives from both the cooperative character of the learning by which wisdom is drawn from experience and the cumulative free acts of commitment and sacrifice which have defined, defended and passed on through time the corporate life of the community.[23]

Ultimately, it bears to us the divine gifts of life, meaning and love, and provides a way both back to their origin and forward to their goal, their *Alpha* and *Omega.*

Reason and Hermeneutics

As the recognition of the value of tradition would appear to constitute a special problem for heirs of the Enlightenment, it may be helpful to reflect briefly on why this is so. Enlightenment rationalism idealizes clarity and distinctness of ideas both in themselves and in their interconnection; as such, it divorces them from their concrete existential and temporal significance. Such an ideal of human knowledge, it is proposed, could be achieved either, as with Descartes, through an intellect working by itself from an intellec tually perceived Archimedean principle or, as with Locke and Carnap, through the senses drawing their ideas exclusively from experience and combining them in myriad tautological transformations.[24] In either case, the result is a-temporal and consequently non-historical knowledge.

Two attempts to break out of this have proven ultimately unsuccessful. One might be termed historist and relativist. In order to recognize historical sequence while retaining the ideal of clarity and distinctness, it attempted to attain detailed knowledge of each period, relativizing everything to its point in time and placing historicity ultimately at the service of the rationalist ideal. The other, the Romantics, ultimately adhered to the same revolutionary Enlightenment ideal even in appearing to oppose it, for, in turning to the past and to myths, they too sought clear and distinct knowledge of a static human nature. Tradition thus became traditionalism, for all was included in the original state of nature and our only way of obtaining a firm grounding for human life was simply to return thereto.

In the rationalist view, in contrast, any meaning not clearly and distinctly perceived was an idol to be smashed (Bacon), an idea to be bracketed by doubt (Descartes), or something to be wiped clean from the slate of the mind as irrational and coercive (Locke and Hume). Any judgment — even if provisional — made before all had been examined and its clarity and distinctness established would be a dangerous imposition by the will.

This points toward the importance of civil society for realizing human life in a manner that reflects and ultimately leads toward the divine. First the enlightenment ideal of absolute knowledge of oneself or of others, simply and without condition, is not possible, for the knower is always conditioned according to his or her position in time and space and in relation to others. But neither would such knowledge be of ultimate interest, for human knowledge, like human beings, develops in time and with others.[25] This does not exclude projects of universal and necessary scientific knowledge, but it does identify these precisely as limited and specialized. They make important but specific, rather than all-controlling, contributions. Hence, other modes of knowledge are required in order to take account of the ongoing and varied life of human freedom and its creative results. Further, this is not a solitary, but a group matter. Hence society, especially civil society, becomes the focus for the appreciation and evaluation of things and for the responses which build our world.

Secondly, according to Descartes,[26] reason is had by all and completely. Therefore, authority could be only an entitlement of some to decide issues by an application of their will, rather than according to an authentic understanding of the truth or justice of an issue. This would be "hastiness" according to Descartes's fourth *Meditation*. Further, the limited number of people in authority means that the vision of which they dispose would be limited by restricted or even individual interests. Finally, as one decision constitutes a precedent for those to follow, authority must become fundamentally bankrupt and hence corruptive.[27]

In this manner, the choice of clarity as an ideal, first by Plato and then by Descartes, has generated an exclusivist mind-set ruled by a reductivist mechanism. It is not only that what is not clear is put aside as irrelevant: Even more, the dynamism whereby we reflect the love by which we have been made and respond to it with openness and generosity comes to be seen in a negative light as cognitively blind, while freedom appears in a negative light as affectively arbitrary. The only way these could achieve a redeeming clarity for the human mind is to be reduced to the unambiguous and simplest viscerial violence of Hobbes's struggle for survival, that is, by being reduced to the animal level where, precisely, human freedom is dispensed with.

In this light, too, there has been a tendency to isolate public authority from the shared moral sense of community. This, in turn, compromises the moral quality of government, which needs to include and be addressed by those who comprehend and share in the social good which government is to address. This we shall see is civil society.

If the cumulative experience of humankind in living together in peace is to make a contribution to the development of modern life, then it will be necessary to return human knowledge to the ongoing lived process of humane discovery and choice in society. This, in turn, takes place within the broad project of human interaction and an active process of reception by one generation of the learning of its predecessors. The emerging consciousness of the importance of this effort has led to broadening the task of hermeneutics from the study of ancient, often biblical, texts to a more inclusive attention to the integral meaning of cultures. There it has found not a mere animal search for survival, but a sense of human dignity which, by transcending survival needs enables human creativity in society and encourages a search for ever higher levels of human life leading ultimately to God.

The reference to the god, Hermes, in the term "hermeneutics" suggests something of the depth of the meaning which is sought throughout human life and its implication for the world of values. The message borne by Hermes is not merely an abstract mathematical formula or a methodological prescription devoid of human meaning and value. Instead, it is the limitless wisdom regarding the source of all and hence its reality and value. Hesiod had appealed for this in the introduction to his *Theogony*: "Hail, children of Zeus! Grant lovely song and celebrate the holy race of the deathless gods who are forever. . . . Tell how at the first gods and earth came to be."[28]

Similarly, Aristotle indicated concern for values and virtues in describing his science of wisdom as "knowing to what end each thing must be done; . . . this end is the good of that thing, and, in general, the supreme good in the whole of nature." Such a science will be most divine, for: "(1) God is thought to be among the causes of all things and to be a first principle, and (2) such a science either God alone can have, or God above all others. All the sciences, indeed, are more necessary than this, but none is better."[29] Rather than evaluating all in terms of reductivist clarity and considering things in a horizontal perspective that is only temporal and totally changing — with an implied relativization of all — hermeneutics or interpretation opens also to a vertical vision of what is highest and deepest in life, most real in itself and most lasting through time. This is the eternal or divine in both being and value, which is the key to mobilizing and orienting the life of society in time.

In this light one is able to understand better the character of religious communities which come together under the inspiration of the Prophets and great examples of the religious life as lived existentially: a Buddha, a Christ or a Muhammad — paradigmatic individuals in A. Cua's term. Each set a distinctive pattern of values and virtues which has been lived through history and unfolded by a community of persons who have attempted singly and together to live the multiple modes of this example. This we will see is a seminal source of the groupings which below will be termed civil society.

At the same time, while still echoing Socrates by searching for the permanent structures of complex entities and the stable laws of change, in redirecting attention to being in time, contemporary attention is open to the essentially temporal character of human-kind and, hence, to the uniqueness of each decision, whether in-dividual or corporate. Thus, hermeneutics attends to the task of translation or interpretation, stressing the presentation to those re-ceiving a message, their historical situation and, hence, the historical character of human life. It directs attention not merely to the pursuit of general truths, but to those to whom truth is expressed, namely, persons in the concrete circumstances of their cultures as these have developed through the history of human interaction with nature, with other human beings and with God. It is this human history as heritage and tradition which sets the circumstances in which one perceives the values presented in the tradition and mobilizes his or her own project toward the future.

Anton T. Cua[30] traces to Vico[31] attention to the unreflective cognitive consensus on common needs and to Shaftesbury[32] the affective sense of common partnership with others that this entails. The result is the synchronic constitution of a community of memory whose members revere and commemorate the same saints and personages who have sacrificed to build or exemplify the community's self image. This results in a community of vision or self-understanding, as well as of hope and expectation. A cultural tradition, in this sense, is the context of the conscious life and striv-ing of a person and of the communities of which one is a member; it is life in its fullest meaning, as past and future, ground and aspira-tion.

In this light, Cua notes that in his *Great Learning* Chu Hsi stresses the importance of investigating the principles at great length until one achieves "a wide and far-reaching penetration (*kuan-t'ung*)." Read as *Kuan-chuan*, this suggests an aesthetic grasp of the unique interconnection of the various components of the *tao* as the unique unifying perspective of the culture. This is not only a contemplative understanding, however, but implies active engagement in the conduct of life. If this be varied by subgroups structured in the patterns of solidarity and subsidiarity of civil society then the accumulation of cooperate life experience, lived according to *li* or ritual propriety and *i* or sense of rightness, emerges from the life of a people as a whole. "For the adherents of the Confucian tradition, the tradition is an object of affection and reverence, largely because the tradition is perceived as an embodiment of wisdom (*chih*), which for Chu Hsi is a repository of insights available for personal and interpersonal appropriation, for coping with present problems and changing circumstances."[33]

The truly important battle at the present time is, then, not between, on the one hand, a chaotic liberalism in which the abstract laws of the marketplace dictate the lives of persons, peoples and nations or, on the other hand, a depersonalizing sense of community in which the dignity of the person is suppressed for an equally abstract utopia. A victory of either would spell disaster. The central battle is, rather, to enable peoples to draw on their heritage, constituted of personal and social assessments and free decisions, and elaborated through the ages by the varied communities as they work out their response to their concrete circumstances. That these circumstances are often shifting and difficult in the extreme is important, but it is of definitive importance that a people's response be truly their own in all their variety and of their society with all its interrelated sub-units. That is, that it be part of their history, of the way they have chosen to order and pattern their social life, and in these terms to shape their free response to the good. This is the character of authority exercised in and by a civil society. It reflects, and indeed is, the freedom being exercised by a people in all the varied groupings in which they have chosen to live and to act.

CULTURAL TRADITIONS AS CREATIVE FREEDOM: THE DIACHRONIC DIMENSION

Thusfar we have considered the exercise of freedom as forming a consistent and integrated pattern of life which constitutes the inheritance or patrinomy of everyone born into a human community. But each generation must live this inheritance in its own time and circumstances and is concerned to pass it on as a patrimony enriched and adapted to its children and children's children in succeeding generation. This process is tradition taken not in the passive sense of receiving, but in the active sense of *tradere* or passing on.

A first requisite for this is a dimension of transcendence. If what we find in the empirical world or even in ourselves is all there is, if this be the extent of being, then our life cannot consist in more than rearranging the elements at our disposition — newness could only be of an accidental character. It is, however, the decisive reality of our life that it is lived in a transcendent context which goes beyond anything finite and indeed is inexhaustible by anything finite. Hence we are always drawn forward and called to radical newness. A tradition then is not a matter of the past, but of new applications. As reflecting the infinite creator and goal this is the decisively religious characterist of human life.

As an active process tradition transforms what is received, lives it in a creative manner and passes it on as a leaven for the future. Let us turn then from the cumulative meaning and value in tradition, its synchronic aspect, to its diachronic or particular meaning for each new time, receiving from the past, ordering the present and constructing the future. This is a matter, first of all, of taking time seriously, that is, of recognizing that reality includes authentic novelty. This contrasts to the perspective of Plato for whom the real is the ideal and unchangeable forms or ideas transcending matter and time, of which physical things and temporal events are but shadows. It also goes beyond rationalism's search for clear and distinct knowledge of eternal and simple natures and their relations in terms of which all might be controlled, as well as beyond romanticism's attention to a primordial unchanging nature hidden in the dimly sensed past. *A fortiori*, it goes beyond method alone without content.

In contrast to all these, the notion of application[34] is based upon an awareness that "reality is temporal and unfolding". This means that tradition, with its inherent authority or normative force, achieves its perfection in the temporal unfolding of reality. Secondly, it shows human persons and social groups, not as detached intellects, but as incarnate and hence enabled by, and formative of, their changing social universe. Thirdly, in the area of socio-political values and action, it expresses directly the striving of persons and groups to realize their lives and the development of this striving into attitudes (*hexis*) and institutions. Hence, as distinct from the physical order, human action is a situation neither of law nor of lawlessness, but of human and, therefore, developing institutions and attitudes.

These do not determine and hence destroy human freedom, but regulate and promote its exercise.[35] This is the heart of civil society for it shows how community and governance can come together.

Certain broad guidelines for the area of ethics and politics serve in the application of tradition as a guide for historical practice and vice-versa. The concrete exercise of human freedom as unique personal decisions made with others in the process of their social life through time constitutes a distinctive and ongoing process. Historicity means that responses to the good are made always in concrete and ever-changing circumstances. Hence, the general principles of ethics and politics as a philosophic science of action cannot be purely theoretical knowledge or a simple accounting from the past. Instead, they must help people consciously exercise their freedom in concrete historical circumstances and groups which change and are renewed.

Here, an important distinction must be made from *techné* where action is governed by an idea as an exemplary cause that is fully determined and known by objective theoretical knowledge (*epistéme*). As in the case of an architect's blueprints, skill, such as that of the engineer, consists in knowing how to act according to that idea or plan. When it cannot be carried out perfectly, some parts of it simply are omitted in the execution. In contrast, civil society and its ethics and politics, though similar in the possession of a practical guide and its application to a particular task, differ in important ways. First, by shared action toward a common goal subjects and especially societies themselves are as much constituted as they produce an object: if agents are differentiated by their action, societies are formed or destroyed by their inner interaction. Hence, moral knowledge, as an understanding of the appropriateness of human action, cannot be fully determined independently of the societies in their situation and in action.

Secondly, adaptation by societies and social groups in their application of the law does not diminish, but rather corrects and perfects the law. In relation to a world which is less ordered, the laws, rules and regulations of groups are imperfect for they cannot contain in any explicit manner the adequate response to the concrete possibilities which arise in history. It is precisely here that the creative freedom of a people is located. It does not consist in arbitrary choice, for Kant is right in saying that without law freedom has no meaning.

Nor does it consist in an automatic response determined by the historical situation, for then determinism and relativism would compete for the crown in undermining human freedom. Freedom consists, rather, in shaping the present according to the sense of what is just and good which we have from our cultural tradition. This we do in a way which manifests and indeed creates for the first time more of what justice and goodness mean.

The law then is not diminished by distinctive and discrete application to the varied parts of a complex civil society, but corrected and enriched. *Epoché* and equity do not diminish, but perfect the law; without them the law would be simply a mechanical replication, doing the work not of justice, but of injustice. Ethics, politics and especially aesthetics which takes account of the unique is then not only knowledge of what is right in general, but the search for what is right for this group or sub-group with its goal and in its situation. Adaptation of the means by the social group, whether occupational, religious or ethnic, is then not a matter of mere expediency. Rather, it is the essence of the search for a more perfect application of a law or tradition in the given situation and therefore the fulfillment of moral knowledge.[36]

It is important to note that this rule of the concrete (of what the situation is asking of us) is not known by sense knowledge, which simply registers a set of concrete facts on the horizontal level. In order to know what is morally required, the situation must be understood in the light of what is right, that is, in the light of what has been discovered vertically through tradition with its normative character about appropriate human action. Only in this light can moral consciousness as the work of intellect (*nous*), rather than of sensation, go about its job of choosing the right means.

Therefore, to proceed simply in reaction to concrete injustices, rather than in the light of one's tradition, is ultimately destructive. It inverts the order just mentioned and results in manipulation of our hopes for the good. Destructive or repressive structures would lead us to the use of correspondingly evil means, suited only to producing evil results. The true response to evil can be worked out only in terms of the good as the highest discovery by a people, passed on in tradition and applied by it in each time and place.

Where there are multiple traditions this must be not a reason for abandoning these humanizing dimensions and proceeding in a lesser manner, but of searching for the ways in which they can be related in a yet more rich and adequate realization of human life.

The importance of application implies a central role for the virtue of prudence (*phronesis*) or thoughtful reflection which enables one to discover the appropriate means for the circumstances. This must include, also, the virtue of sagacity (*sunesis*), that is, of understanding or concern for the other. For what is required as a guide for the agent is not only the technical knowledge of an abstract ideal, but knowledge that takes account of the agent in relation to other persons. One can assess the situation adequately only inasmuch as one, in a sense, undergoes the situation with the affected parties, living and suffering with them. Aristotle rightly describes as "terrible" the one who is capable of manipulating the situation, but is without orientation towards moral ends and without concern for the good of others in their concrete situations.

In sum, application is not a subsequent or accidental part of understanding, added on after perfect understanding has been achieved; rather it co-determines this understanding from the beginning. Moral consciousness must seek to understand the good, not as an ideal to be known and then applied, but rather through discerning the good for concrete peoples in their relations with others.

Cua finds similar notions in the distinctions of Chu Hsi in the neo-Confucian tradition regarding the diachronic sense of *tao* as residing between the substantial (*t'i*) and the operational (*yung*), the stable basic or latent schemata and its operational sense in changing circumstances (*fei*). Hsün Tzu distinguishes the constant (*ch'ang*) and the changing (*pien*), and Mencius the constant rule (*ching*) and the sliding scale (*ch'üuan*). Use of the latter as an exercise of moral discretion based on *li* is essential for moral life due to the imperfections of our knowledge and the urgent complexity of life. In these circumstances, to hold to a static mean would undermine the realization of the holistic goal of the *tao*.

Creativity in the application of the tradition in the concrete circumstances of life thus becomes essential. In this context Cua cites J. Pelican's deft aphorism: "Tradition is the living faith of the dead, traditionalism is the dead faith of the living."[37]

METAPHYSICAL AND RELIGIOUS ROOTS
OF TRADITIONS

The notion of application can help in sorting out the human dilemma between an absolutism insensitive to persons in their concrete circumstances and a relativism which leaves the person subject to expediency in public and private life. Indeed, the very statement of the dilemma reflects the deleterious aspect of the Platonic view of ideas. He was right to ground changing and historical being in the unchanging and eternal. This had been Parmenides's first insight in metaphysics and has been richly developed in relation to human action through the medievals' notion of an eternal law in the divine mind.

But it seems inappropriate to speak directly in these terms regarding human life, for in all things individual human persons and humankind as a whole are subject to time, growth and development. As we become increasingly conscious of this, the personal character even of our abstract ideals becomes manifest and their adapted application in time can be seen, not as their rejection, but as their perfection. In this, justice loses none of its force as an absolute requirement of human action. Rather, the concrete modes of its application in particular circumstances add to what might have been articulated in merely abstract and universal terms. A hermeneutic approach directs attention precisely to these unfoldings of the meaning of abstract principles through time. This is not an abandonment of absolutes, but a recognition of the human condition and of the way in which this continually and, in endlessly marvelous manners, unfolds the ultimate richness of the source and goal, and hence the principles, of social life.

For Confucius, the aesthetic vision is integrated in drama, of which dance is one moment. In the actual performance of *li* (ritual or liturgy), there is a combination of poetry, liturgical action and music. Confucius saw that in the poem our spirit can rise and achieve complete transcendence in the ecstasy of the spirit. This gives access in aesthetic terms to a source, not only of inspiration, but of vision that both draws one to aspire to greater perfection and opens the way for creative thought regarding ways in which this can be achieved.

Some suggest, however, that Confucius may have looked upon

aesthetics more as a matter of appreciation and conservation, rather than as original, creative and free expression. This suggests that, in the works of Confucius, there are resources important for developing a modern vision which were unmined by Confucius himself and his schools.

If so what should be the attitude of a philosopher in our day to this mode of aesthetics? If it be itself appreciative and conservative, is one who interprets it subject to the same approach and limited to the same content, or can interpretation legitimately open up new meaning in old texts? In other words, must ancient texts be read only with an ancient outlook? Indeed, is it even possible today to have an authentically ancient outlook — to see with eyes long closed in death — or does the attempt to do so require so much make-believe as to be in effect impossible? Even if one were to succeed in reconstituting the past, would one be faithful to the text which was written as a vital expression of the process of life, or would one instead be rendering lifeless a living text[38] (not unlike the biologist who makes a slide of once living tissue)?

It would seem, therefore, that our goal should be not simply to reiterate ancient times in reading ancient texts, but to recognize that we come to them from new times, with new horizons and new questions. We should allow them to speak anew to us; in so doing, the texts and philosophies are living rather than dead — and, therefore, more true. Texts read in this sense are part of a living tradition in which is situated our struggle to face the problems of life and build a future worthy of those who follow.

Some would fear that to give such importance to the horizon of the reader of a text might constitute a relativism and lose the permanent significance of the insights of the author. But this would seem to reflect a material and mechanical model ruled by successive discrete moments of time in which universality is a function only of abstraction. This leaves what is universally applicable as relatively vacuous and reduces one to pragmatism as one's only response to concrete and changing circumstances.

Here, the real issue regards one's metaphysics: what is the nature of being, what does it mean to be? If the answer, as the Confucian sense of community would be the first to suggest, is not that reality is reductively matter trapped in time but at least the human spirit living through time, then to look for meaning in terms of the reaches of the spirit across time is not to lose, but to find meaning. This is the sense of being emerging through the conscious-ness of Heidegger's person as *dasein*. Being is not merely what was, but what blossoms ever fresh in the human heart. In the same way, philosophy in reading ancient texts is not archeology but, like every human act, a creative unfolding of being in time. This creative freedom is the essential characteristic of the person.[39]

Moreover, it is precisely as this is seen in the context of an understanding of being as infinite and transcending that we are opened beyond ourselves and even beyond the present state of society.

Our mind and heart are directed toward an inner transcendence, Being itself which is the source from which the dasein emerges into time. This was the dynamic of the investigations of Heidegger as he moved from his earlier period of *Being in Time* to the so-called later Heidegger which concentrated rather on Being itself, the infinite source of all beings. As the source of precisely of our conscious intentional life this is Spirit marked not only by conscious self-awareness but celebrating its own perfection in and as love Shankara at the heart of the Hindu religious tradition would express this by his advaitan (or non-dualist) metaphysics of the absolute as existence, consciousness and bliss. This Christian sense of creation would express it is the life of the Spirit not only as creative source and ultimate goal (alpha and omega) but as lived by persons and peoples, individually and socially in the exercise of responsible freedom through time. We are moved thereby to pursue the realization in time of a social life reflecting the Unity, Truth and Goodness of the divine in which being is founded and life consists. In this lies stimulation for progress and hope for success.

What, then, should we conclude regarding the root of the actuality, the good or the perfection of reality which mankind has discovered, in which we have been raised, which gives us dominion over our actions, and which enables us to be free and creative? Does it come from God or from man, from eternity or from history? Chakravarti Rajagopalachari of Madras answered:

> Whether the epics and songs of a nation spring from
> the faith and ideas of the common folk, or whether
> a nation's faith and ideas are produced by its

literature is a question which one is free to answer
as one likes. . . . Did clouds rise from the sea or
was the sea filled by waters from the sky? All such
inquiries take us to the feet of God transcending
speech and thought.[40]

Religious Pluralism and the Progress of Cultures and Civilizations

We encounter here an issue especially pregnant for progress
in our time of globalization and interchange between cultures and
civilizations. That is, if the diachronic character of tradition as
prospective and progressive is founded in the Transcendent
articulated explicitly in their religions how can the religious traditions
themselves find a fidelity that is progressive.

Thus far, we have treated the character and importance of
tradition as bearing the long experience of persons interacting with
their world, with other persons and with God. It is made up not only
of chronological facts, but of insights regarding human perfection
and its foundations which have been forged by human efforts in
concrete circumstances, e.g., the Greek notion of democracy and
the Enlightenment notions of equality and freedom. By their internal
value, these stand as normative of the aspirations of a people.

Secondly, we have seen the implication of historicity for
novelty within the context of tradition, namely, that the continually
unfolding circumstances of historical development not merely extend
or repeat what went before, but constitute an emerging manifestation
of the divine roots of being that is articulated by the art, religion,
literature and political structures of a cultural tradition.

It remains for us now to treat the third element in this study
of tradition, namely, to see how the hermeneutic method can
contribute to enabling the religious roots of cultures to be unfolded
through mutually questioning to contribute to the progress of
humankind. That is, we have seen how synchronically the infinite
and eternal perfection of God be participated in patterns that
constitute by persons, cultures lived in th many groupings of a civil
society. We have seen also how diachronically these cultural
traditions are mere prospective than retrospective when unfolded
in ways that are relevant, indicative and directive of our life in

present circumstances? Thirdly we have seen how the potentiality for this rich adaptive character of tradition lies in their transcendent and religious roots. Now we must see how can the two of these combine so that the religious foundations of the many peoples interact in a way that enables each and all to proceed jointly to facing the future?

The Hermeneutics of a Cultural Tradition: Unfolding by Questioning

If we take time and culture seriously, then we must recognize that we are situated in a particular culture and at a particular time. All that can be seen from this vantage point constitutes one's horizon. This would be lifeless and dead, determined rather than free, if our vantage point were to be fixed by its circumstances and closed. Hence we need to meet other minds and hearts not simply to add information incrementally, but to be challenged in our basic assumptions and enabled thereby to delve more deeply into our tradition and draw forth deeper and more pervasive truth. How can this be done?

First of all, it is necessary to note that only a unity of meaning, that is, an identity, is intelligible.[41] Just as it is not possible to understand a number five if we include only four units rather than five, no act of understanding is possible unless it is directed to an identity or whole of meaning. This brings us to the classic issue of the hermeneutic circle in which knowledge of the whole depends upon knowledge of the parts, and vice versa. How can this work for, rather than against, the development of social life?

The experience of reading a text might be suggestive. As we read we construe the meaning of a sentence before grasping all its individual parts. What we construe is dependent upon our expectation of the meaning of the sentence, which we derived from its first words, the prior context, or more likely, from a combination of the two. In turn, our expectation or construal of the meaning of the text is adjusted according to the requirements of its various parts as we proceed to read through the parts of the sentence, the paragraph, etc., continually reassessing the whole in terms of the parts and the parts in terms of the whole. This basically circular movement continues until all appears to fit and to be clear.

Similarly, in regard to our cultural tradition and values, we develop a prior conception of its content. This anticipation of meaning is not simply of the tradition as an objective past or fixed content to which we come; it is rather what we produce as we participate in the evolution of the tradition and, thereby, further determine ourselves. This is a creative stance reflecting the content, not only of the past, but of the time in which I stand and of the life project in which I am engaged. It is a creative unveiling of the content of the tradition as this comes progressively and historically into the present and through the present, passes into the future.

In this light, time is not a barrier, separation or abyss, but rather a bridge and opportunity for the process of understanding, a fertile ground filled with experience, custom and tradition. The importance of the historical distance it provides is not that it enables the subjective reality of persons to disappear so that the objectivity of the situation can emerge. On the contrary, it makes possible a more complete meaning of the tradition, less by removing falsifying factors than by opening new sources of self-understanding which reveal in the tradition unsuspected implications and even new dimensions of meaning.[42]

Of course, not all our acts of understanding about the meaning of a text from another culture, a dimension of a shared tradition, a set of goals or a plan for future action are sufficient. Hence, it becomes particularly important that they not be adhered to fixedly, but be put at risk in dialogue with others.

In this, the basic elements remain the substances or persons which Aristotle described in terms of autonomy and, by implication, of identity. Hermeneutics would expand this to reflect as well the historical and hermeneutic situation of each person in the dialogue, that is, their horizon or particular possibility for understanding. As an horizon is all that can be seen from one's vantage point(s), in dialogue with others it is necessary to be aware of our horizon, as well as that of others. For it is precisely when our initial projection of their meaning will not bear up under the progressive dialogue that we are required to make needed adjustments in our projection of their meaning.

This enables one to adjust one's prior understanding not only of the horizon of the other with whom one is in dialogue, but especially of one's own horizon. Hence, one need not fear being trapped; horizons are vantage points of a mind which in principle is open and mobile, capable of being aware of its own limits and of transcending them through acknowledging the horizons of others. The flow of history implies that we are not bound by our horizons, but move in and out of them. It is in making us aware of our horizons that hermeneutic consciousness accomplishes our liberation.[43]

For this, we must maintain a questioning attitude. Rather than simply following through with our previous ideas until a change is forced upon us, we must remain sensitive to new meanings in true openness. This is neither neutrality as regards the meaning of the tradition, nor an extinction of passionate concerns regarding action towards the future. Rather, being aware of our own biases or prejudices and adjusting them in dialogue with others implies rejecting what impedes our understanding of others or of traditions. Our attitude in approaching dialogue must be one of willingness continually to revise our initial projection or expectation of meaning.

The way out of the hermeneutic circle is then not by ignoring or denying our horizons and initial judgments or prejudices, but by recognizing them as inevitable and making them work for us in drawing out, not the meaning of the text for its author,[44] but its application for the present. Through this process of application we serve as midwife for culture as historical or tradition, enabling it to give birth to the future.[45]

The logical structure of this process is the exchange of question and answer. A question is required in order to determine just what issue we are engaging — whether it is this issue or that — so that we might give direction to our attention. Without this, no meaningful answer can be given or received. As a question, however, it requires that the answer not be settled or determined. In sum, progress or discovery requires an openness which is not simple indeterminacy, but a question which gives specific direction to our attention and enables us to consider significant evidence.

If discovery depends upon the question, then the art of discovery is the art of questioning. Consequently, in working in conjunction with others, the heart of the democratic process is not to suppress, but to reinforce and unfold the questions of others. To the degree that these probabilities are built up and intensified they can serve as a searchlight. This is the opposite of both opinion which tends to suppress questions, and of arguing which searches out the weakness in the other's positions. Instead, in democracy, understood as conversation and dialogue directed toward governance, one enters upon a mutual search to maximize the possibilities of the question, even by speaking at cross purposes, for it is by mutually eliminating errors and working out a common meaning that we discover truth.[46]

In this there appears the importance of interreligious dialogue. Rather than being merely an external act of mutual acknowledgement, in view of what has been said above it is a true requisite if our cultures are to be open and developing. As religion is the basic conscious recognition of the transcendent horizon which invites progress, interchange between religions is important in order that this relation of cultures to their infinite source and goal remain open and be renewed. Indeed this would seem to be the more important the more education especially in its modern rationalist context advances, for the more a tradition is rationalized, philosophized or theologized the more it is made stable and fixed, and the greater the danger of its becoming closed in upon itself and becoming inadequate for its task of reflecting the infinite and transcendent.

Religious Pluralism: Dialogue and Progress

Further, in the present context of globalization such interchange provides an alternative to the much feared conflict of civilizations projected by S. Huntington. It should not be presupposed that a text, such as a tradition, law or constitution, will hold the answer to but one question or can have but one horizon which must be identified by the reader. On the contrary, the full horizon of the author(s) is never available to the reader, nor can it be expected that there is but one question to which a tradition or document holds an answer. The sense of texts reaches beyond what their authors intended because the dynamic character of being as it emerges in time means that the horizon is never fixed but is continually opening. This constitutes the effective historical element in understanding a text or a tradition. At each step new dimensions of its potentialities open to understanding, so that the meaning of a text or tradition lives with the consciousness and hence the horizons — not of its author — but of people in dialogue with others through time and history.

This is the essence both of democracy within a nation and of globalization between peoples. They are processes of broadening horizons, through fusion with the horizons of others in dialogue, that makes it possible for each to receive from one's cultural tradition and its values answers which are ever new.[47]

In this, one's personal attitudes and interests remain important. If our interest in developing new horizons is simply the promotion of our own understanding then we could be interested solely in achieving knowledge, and thereby in domination over others. This would lock one into an absoluteness of one's prejudices; being fixed or closed in the past, they would disallow new life in the present. In this manner, powerful new insights can become with time deadening pre-judgments which suppress freedom. This would seem to be the suppositive of Samuel Huntington's *Clash of Civilizations*. He sees civilizations as grounded in religions and develops at length the reason for the expectation that these will become ever more influential as time progresses. Unfortunately he sees all identities as essentially self-centered and conflictual.

In contrast, an attitude of authentic religion as well as of democratic openness appreciates the nature of one's own finiteness. This has two dimensions. One is that of time, by which one able at once to respect the past and to be open to discerning the future. Such openness is a matter of recognizing the historical nature of man and his basis in an Absolute that transcends and grounds time. The other dimension is horizontal, across civilizations, cultures and their religious foundations. This too is based in the absolute which no culture can adequately reflect. This enables us to escape fascination with externals and deliver more deeply into the deeper reaches of religious awareness by learning from other's experiences.[48]

This suggests that openness does not consist in surveying others objectively, obeying them in a slavish and unquestioning manner or simply juxtaposing their ideas and traditions to our own. Rather, it is directed primarily to ourselves, for our ability to listen to others is correlatively our ability to assimilate the implications of their answers for delving more deeply into the meaning of our own traditions and drawing out new and ever more rich insights. In other words, it is an acknowledgement that our cultural heritage has something new to say to us.

The characteristic hermeneutic attitude of effective historical consciousness is, then, not methodological sureness, readiness for new compromises or new techniques of social organization, for these are subject to social critique and manipulation on the horizontal level. Instead, it is readiness to draw out in democratic dialogue new meaning from a common tradition.[49] Seen in these terms our heritage of culture and values is not closed or dead, but, through a democratic life, remains ever new by becoming even more inclusive and more rich.

This takes us beyond the rigid rationalism of the civil society of the later Enlightenment and the too fluid moral sentiment of the earlier Enlightenment. It enables us to respond to the emerging sense of the identity of peoples and to protect and promote this in a civil society marked by solidarity and subsidiarity.

In this as a social work one guiding principle is to maintain a harmony or social equilibrium through time. In addition the notion of application allows the tradition to provide resources and guidance in facing new issues and in developing new responses to changing times. With rising numbers and expectations, economic development becomes an urgent need. But its very success could turn into defeat if this is not oriented and applied with a pervasive but subtle and adaptive human governance sensitive to all forms of human comity. This is required in order to orient all suavely to the social good in which the goal of civil society consists.

This will require new advances in science and economics, in education and psychology, in the humanities and social services, that is, across the full range of social life. All these dimensions, and many more, must spring to new life, but in a basic convergence and harmony. The values and virtues emerging from a religiously grounded tradition applied in a freedom can provide needed guidance along new and ever evolving paths. In this way cooperation between religions can be a key to social progress.

Cooperation among Cultures and Civilizations
as a Religious Thanksgiving

Thus far we have articulated the cultural tradition as emerging from human experience and creativity in the exercise of human life, both personally and in the social groups which constitute a civil society. We have seen also how the force of this reflects its foundation in the absolute unity, truth and love of the divine in time.

That sense of gift may make it possible to extend the notions of duty and harmony beyond concern for the well-being of myself and those with whom I share, and whose well-being is then in a sense my own. The good is not only what contributes to my perfection, for I am not the center of meaning. Rather, being as received is essentially out-going.

This has two important implications for our topic. Where the Greek focus upon their own heritage had led to depreciating others as barbarians, the sense of oneself and of one's culture as radically given or gifted provides a basic corrective. Knowing and valuing oneself and one's culture as gifts implies more than merely reciprocating what the other does for me. It means, first, that others and their culture are to be respected simply because they too have been given or gifted by the one transcendent source. This is an essential step which Gandhi, in calling outcasts by the name "harijans" or "children of God," urged us to take beyond the sense of pride or isolation in which we would see others in pejorative terms.

But mere respect is not enough. The fact that I and another — my people or culture and another — originate from, share in and proclaim the same "total absolute", especially as this creates not out of need but out of love, implies that the relation between cultures as integrating modes of human life is in principle one of complementarity and out reach. Hence, interchange as the effort to live this complementarity is far from being hopeless. In the pressing needs of our times only an intensification of bonds of cooperation between peoples can make available the needed immense stores of human experience and creativity. The positive virtue of love is our real basis for hope.

A second principle of interchange is to be found in the participated — the radically given or gifted — character of one's being. One does not first exist and then receive, but one's very existence is a received existence or gift. To attempt to give back this gift, as in an exchange of presents, would be at once hopelessly too much and too little. On the one hand, to attempt to return in strict equivalence would be too much, for it is our very self that we have received as gift. On the other hand, to think merely in terms of reciprocity would be to fall essentially short of one's nature as one that is given, for to make a merely equivalent return would be to remain centered upon oneself where one would cleverly trap, and then entomb, the creative power of being.

Rather, looking back one can see the futility of giving back, and in this find the fundamental importance of passing on the gift in the spirit in which it has been received. One's nature as given calls for a creative generosity which reflects that of its source. Truly appropriate generosity lies in continuing the giving of which I have received. This means shaping one's cultural tradition creatively in response to the present needs not only of ourselves but of others, and cooperating with the creative gifts at the heart of other cultures so that they may be fully lived and shared.

This religious vision requires a vast expansion or breaking out of oneself as the only center of one's concern. It means becoming appreciative and effectively concerned with the good of others and of other groups, with the promotion and vital growth of the next generation and those to follow. This is the motivation to engage with others in the creation of a civil society and to contribute thereby to the good of the whole. Indeed it means advancing Iqbal's insight regarding religious thought a step further to a total harmony of man and nature which reflects the total absolute as the condition of possibility of all.

CONCLUSION: THE RELIGIOUS RECONSTRUCTION OF LIFE IN OUR TIMES

The implications of such generosity are broad and at times surprisingly personal. First, true openness to others cannot be based upon a depreciation of oneself or of one's own culture. Without appreciating one's worth there would be nothing to share and no way to help, nor even the possibility of enjoying the good of the other. Further, cultural interchange enables one to see that elements of one's life, which in isolation may have seemed to be merely local customs and purely repetitive in character, more fundamentally are modes in which one lives basic and essential human values. In meeting others and other cultures, one discovers the deeper meaning in one's own everyday life.

One does more than discover, however. One recognizes that

in these transcendental values of life — truth and freedom, love
and beauty — one participates in the dynamism of one's origin and
hence must share these values in turn. More exactly, one comes to
realize that real reception of these transcendental gifts lies in
sharing them in loving concern in order that others may realize them
as well. This means passing on one's own heritage not by replicating
it in others, but by promoting what others and subsequent generations
would freely become.

Finally, that other cultures are quintessentially products of self-
cultivation by other spirits as free and creative images of their divine
source implies the need to open one's horizons beyond one's own
self-concerns to the ambit of the freedom of others. This involves
promoting the development of other free and creative centers and
cultures which, precisely as such, are not in one's own possession
or under one's own control. One lives then no longer in terms merely
of oneself or of things that one can make or manage, but in terms of
an interchange between free persons and people's of different
cultures. Personal responsibility is no longer merely individual decision making or for individual good. Effectively realized, the resulting
interaction and mutual fecundation reaches out beyond oneself and
one's own culture to reflect ever more perfectly the glory of the
one source and goal of all.[50]

This calls for a truly shared effort in which all respond fully,
not only to majority or even common needs, but to the particular
needs of each. This broad sense of tolerance and loving outreach
even in the midst of tensions is the fruit of Iqbal's religious attitude
of appreciation as mediated through a phenomenology of gift. It
has been described by Pope John Paul II as a state in which violence
cedes to peaceful transformation, and conflict to pardon and reconciliation; where power is made reasonable by persuasion, and justice
finally is implemented through love.[51]

There is an image for this in the Book of Isaiah. It is that of
the many nations, each proceeding along its own way marked out
by its own culture, and all converging toward the Holy Mountain in
which God will become All in all.[52] Today we are conscious of and
effected by this process not only in the lives of our own people and
civilization but in others as well. Here have tried to see how this
can be a process of enrichment which does not destroy but evolves
our own identity and that that process in turn depends upon and

contributes to others. In this the lyncheine is transcendence: the ability to open by interchange with others to more of the resources of our culture and conversely by going more deeply into our own identity to find its relation to others. This is the hermeneutic interchange of whole and part in which we are the actors, the life of humankind is the text and religion is its foundation.

NOTES

1. John Locke, *An Essay Concerning Human Understanding* (New York: Dover, 1959), Book II, chap. I, vol. I; 121-124.

2. David Hume, *An Enquiry Concerning Human Understanding* (Chicago: Regnery, 1960).

3. R. Carnap, *Vienna Manifesto*, trans. A. Blumberg in G. Kreyche and J. Mann, *Perspectives on Reality* (New York: Harcourt, Brace and World, 1966), p. 485.

4. *The Theory of Justice* (Cambridge: Harvard University Press, 1971).

5. M. Adler, *The Idea of Freedom: A Dialectical Examination of the Conceptions of Freedom* (Garden City, NJ: Doubleday, 1958), I, 62.

6. Ivor Leclerc, "The Metaphysics of the Good," *Review of Metaphysics*, 35 (1981), 3-5.

7. *Laches*, 198-201.

8. *Nichomachean Ethics*, VII, 9, 1159b25-1160a30.

9. Gerald F. Stanley, "Contemplation as Fulfillment of the Human Person," in *Personalist Ethics and Human Subjectivity*, vol. II of *Ethics at the Crossroads*, George F. McLean, ed (Washington: The Council for Research in Values and Philosophy, 1996), pp. 365-420.

9. J.L. Mehta, *Martin Heidegger: The Way and the Vision* (Honolulu: University of Hawaii Press, 1976), pp. 90-91.

10. V. Mathieu, "Cultura" in *Enciclopedia Filosofica* (Firenze: Sansoni, 1967), II, 207-210; and Raymond Williams, "Culture and Civilization," *Encyclopedia of Philosophy* (New York: Macmillan, 1967), II, 273-276, and *Culture and Society* (London, 1958).

12. Tonnelat, "Kultur" in *Civilisation, le mot et l'idée* (Paris:

Centre International de Synthese), II.

13. V. Mathieu, *ibid.*

14. V. Mathieu, "Civilta," *ibid.*, I, 1437-1439.

15. G.F. Klemm, *Allgemein Culturgeschicht der Menschheit* (Leipzig, 1843-1852), x.

16. E.B. Tylor, *Primitive Culture* (London, 1871), VII, p. 7.

17. Clifford Geertz, *The Interpretation of Cultures* (London: Hutchinson, 1973), p. 5.

18. *Ibid.*, p. 10.

19. *Ibid.*, p. 13.

20. *Ibid.*, p. 85.

21. John Caputo, "A Phenomenology of Moral Sensibility: Moral Emotion," in George F. McLean, Frederick Ellrod, eds., *Philosophical Foundations for Moral Education and Character Development: Act and Agent* (Washington: The Council for Research in Values and Philosophy, 1992), pp. 199-222.

22. Gadamer, pp. 245-53; Muhammed Iqbal, *The Reconstruction of Religious Thought in Islam* (Lahore: Iqbal Academy, 1989).

23. *Ibid.* Gadamer emphasizes knowledge as the basis of tradition in contrast to those who would see it pejoratively as the result of arbitrary will. It is important to add to knowledge the free acts which, e.g., give birth to a nation and shape the attitudes and values of successive generations. As an example one might cite the continuing impact had by the Magna Carta through the Declaration of Independence upon life in North America, or of the Declaration of the Rights of Man in the national life of so many countries.

24. R. Carnap.

25. H. G. Gadamer, *Truth and Method* (New York: Crossroads, 1975), pp. 305-310.

26. R. Descartes, *Discourse on Method*, I.

27. Gadamer, pp. 240, 246-247.

28. Hesiod, *Theogony* trans. H.G. Everland-White (Loeb Classical Lib.; Cambridge, Mass.: Harvard Univ. Press, 1964), p. 85.

29. Aristotle, *Metaphysics*, I, 2.

30. "The Idea of Confucian Tradition," *The Review of Metaphysics*, XLV (1992), 803-840.

31. Giambattista Vico, *The New Science*, trans. T. Bergin

and M Fisch (Ithica: Cornell Univ. Press, 1988).

32. *Characteristics of Men, Manners, Opinions, Times,* ed. Robertson (Indianapolis: Bobbs-Merrill, 1964), Vol. I, p. 72.

33. "Confucian Tradition" and "Hsun Tsu and the Unity of Virtues," *Journal of Chinese Philosophy,* 14 (1978), 92-94.

34. Gadamer, pp. 281-286.

35. *Ibid.,* pp. 278-279.

36. *Ibid.,* pp. 281-286.

37. Jaroslav Pelican, *Vindication of Tradition* (New Haven: Yale University Press, 1984), p. 65.

38. B. Tatar, *Interpretation and the Problem of the Intention of the Author: H.-G. Gadamer vs E.D. Hirsch* (Washington: The Council for Research in Values and Philosophy, 1998).

39. Musa Dibadj, *The Authenticity of the Text in Hermeneutics* (Washington: The Council for Research in Values and Philosophy, 1998).

40. *Ramayana* (Bombay: Bharatiya Vidya Bhavan, 1976), p. 312.

41. Gadamer, p. 262.

42. *Ibid.,* pp. 263-64.

43. *Ibid.,* pp. 235-242, 267-271.

44. B. Tatar.

45. Gadamer, pp. 235-332.

46. *Ibid.,* pp. 225-332.

47. *Ibid.,* pp. 336-340.

48. *Ibid.,* pp. 327-324.

49. *Ibid.,* pp. 324-325.

50. Schmitz, pp. 84-86.

51. John Paul II, "Address at Puebla," *Origins,* VIII (n.34, 1979), I, 4 and II, 41-46.

52. *Isaiah* 27:13.

CHAPTER II

CULTURAL TRADITIONS AS PROSPECTIVE AND PROGRESSIVE: THE DIACHRONIC DIMENSION
(Tashkent Lecture)

Tradition as Synchronic

The first lecture distinguished three levels of freedom: (a) to choose as I want, (b) to choose as I ought, and (c) to construct one's life project in the common good. It directed attention especially to the third, creative or existential life project and the way in which over time a people develops a culture and a cultural tradition. This involves the exercise of freedom in concrete circumstances which develops a pattern of values and of virtues that coalesce to constitute a consistent whole. This is tradition taken cumulatively and synchronically. The ethics of Aristotle may be thought of as just this — a pattern of virtues constituting a consistent whole for practical action and the exercise of life.

His study of the social application and implementation of this ethics constitutes his *Politics*. There he developed the notion of governance as basically a matter of freedom understood as *arché*, to which he adds to the virtues of friendship for solidarity and subsidiarity. This provides the basic architecture of the social life of a culture in which people coalesce in groups according to their interests and capabilities for the common good. The result as passed through time constitutes a tradition into which people are born and which they receive as a good way to live.

In modern times the notion of civil society was developed especially by the Scottish philosophers, Adam Smith and Adam Fergerson. Today civil society often is thought of in terms of those Scottish origins or in terms of its theoretical elaboration on the continent by Hegel and Marx. The issue of civil society was raised by the Chinese philosophers in the series of annual joint colloquia sponsored jointly with The Council for Research in Values and Philosophy. But if they sensed the need to follow the opening of the market by a corresponding development of civil society, it is not probable that they can or would want to model themselves on the Scots of two centuries ago or on the Europeans a bit later. If civil society is to be an exercise of the freedom of a people it must be developed on their own basis, in terms of their own values and virtues, and hence of their own cultural tradition. Hence the opening paper for the colloquium with the Chinese on civil society began with Aristotle and followed with a history of the modern European notions of civil society. But the second half of the paper was entitled: "Opening a new space for civil society". This developed the sense of the cultural tradition of a people as providing the basis for the orientation of its public life.

Its implication is that each people must look into its own tradition as the basis for the development of its pattern of civil life. That begins from below in the groupings of the people and on the basis of their exercise of freedom gradually builds a pattern for democratic participation.

But here a central question emerges: Is tradition a barrier to progress? Indeed, if one sees life only in terms of the first level of freedom as consisting in random choices between external objects any prior commitments or orientations can be seen as impediments. Hence, it becomes the not too subtle project of a liberal market economy, which would totally control peoples lives, to see that nothing orients the choice of objects to be purchased other than the advertising media. Any advance to further levels of freedom concerned with choosing as I ought or allowing for the concerns of a life project that goes beyond economic profit is considered by that ideology a threat to be suppressed by all means. Perceived in these terms it is possible for some to see the development of a cultural tradition as a barrier to "progress."

Conversely, it is the task of an enlightened business ethics to see how values and social concerns relate positively to economic progress. Here our task will be to confront the issue directly and to reexamine the notion of tradition, this time not only as a synchronic pattern of cumulative freedom, but as a diachronic project for a people and a society. Hence I would turn now to tradition as the basis for progress.

Tradition as Diachronic and Prospective

Our problem today is how to move from a strong concentration of power which seemed to depersonalize life without moving to the other side of the Cold War, namely, a chaotic struggle ruled by the equally depersonalizing laws of the market. In other words can we engage the exercise of freedom in the development of values and virtues by a people based on their history with their commitments. This must be done in a way that does not point into the past, but rather provides a basis for a creative and prospective project for the future.

This is a philosophical problem on which work by teams of philosophers today, each in their own context, is indispensable and urgent. It is the issue of time as a characteristic of human life lived not ideologically but existentially. It is the appreciation that time means not just an empty frame that measures anything, nor mere repetition of the same events, but the development of authentic newness or novelty that is the essence of human life as project. Human tradition has its perfection not in the past as something fixed and static, but as the unfolding or blossoming of reality through the free exercise of life in our time and by our creativity.

What is important here is recognition of the reality of the temporal, that is, of authentic novelty. One would think that for us temporal beings this would be obvious. But as humans we are in the ambiguous position of being at once responsible to the whole and engaged in the particular. Indeed it might be said that this is the heart of the human reality and of the whole of creation. Our glory is that we can reach out to the whole of being and meaning in its highest, eternal and infinite realization and in these terms engage in the delicate yet momentous uniqueness of the exercise of responsible freedom.

For this, many steps in philosophy, while of vital importance in themselves, remain insufficient. For Plato's unchangeable forms the temporal was only a shadow. For rationalism's search for the clear and distinct what was real was the abstract, eternal and unchangeable natures and laws. For the romantic it was the ideal past. For yet others, most common in our day, it is method or process without content.

In contrast, human tradition has its perfection not in the past, but as the temporal unfolding of reality. Human persons and groups are not detached intellects grasping abstractly at laws or patterns, but incarnate in matter and time and both forming and enabled by their changing social universe. Hence, socio-political values express the striving of people to realize their lives. These must be formed into institutions which do not destroy human freedom, but regulate and promote its exercise.

In this light the reality and reason of human freedom is not arbitrary choice — as Kant noted freedom requires law for its rational orientation — nor is it determinism either from the historical or economic situation or even from tradition. Instead the work of freedom is the shaping of the present according to the sense of what is just and good. This is discovered in and from the cultural tradition, considered not so much as a horizontal project of sequential trial and error, but as a vertical ever deeper penetration into what justice and goodness mean.

Marx was very concerned with the ongoing dialectical process. But he may have tried too hard to develop a scientific notion of progress. For in so doing he identified necessary laws of human history, but did not allow adequately for the distinctive activity of each person and people to contribute to this ongoing process.

This is not a new phenomenon. Spinoza tried to develop freedom in a rationalist context; Leibriz tried again. Both failed because they tried too hard to impose the clarity of human reason on a human life which was much more creative, rich and varied. Hence, they did not succeed in allowing for the full dynamism of human freedom.

The task of the third sense of human freedom, that is, freedom as an existential project is then neither to develop a realm of arbitrary choice nor to develop a realm of determinism, but rather to shape the present according to the sense of what is just and good which has been discovered by a people in their cultural tradition, and to do this in a way that enables them to continue to manifest more of what justice and goodness mean.

In the hermeneutics made possible by the recent development of phenomenology there are helpful ideas regarding the application to the present of vision developed in the past. This does not mean that we have a clearly defined objective notion of justice which, like a blueprint, we simply replicate in the same way at each time, no matter what the circumstance. Rather we have a sense of the all pervading importance of justice which is not an empirical observation, but truly the work of the intellect. Through time and the experience of humankind, human consciousness goes more deeply into what life is about and finds the importance of it being lived with justice, love, etc.

This is not the same as seeing ahead of time all that life implies and entails — to do so would kill freedom and make human life simply the automatic unfolding of an abstract formula. That was the limitation of even dialectical utopias which suppressed freedom. It is the limitation as well of attempts to spell out marriage agreements in legal documents. Instead marriage is contracted in opposite terms: in sickness or health, for richer or poorer — that is, in whatever circumstances one promises to love and cherish one's partner.

Thus justice and love are appreciated, honored and valued and can be a strong directive force in the social exercise of freedom whenever they can be convincingly appealed to and applied.

An example of this in Washington is the memorial to Abraham Lincoln, who freed the slaves almost 150 years ago. His memorial expresses ideal of justice and equality inherent in the whole American experience. In the 1960s when the black people of the country felt that they had not received justice and were unfairly treated and demeaned, Martin Luther King assembled a huge group, black and white, before the Lincoln Memorial. There he gave a speech, at the end of which he said:

> I have a dream that one day this nation will rise up and live out the true meaning of its creed: "We hold these truths to be self-evident: that all men are created equal."
>
> . . .
>
> I have a dream that one day every valley shall be exalted, every hill and mountain shall be made low, the rough places will be made plain, and the crooked places will be made straight, and the glory of the Lord shall be revealed, and all flesh shall see it together.
>
> . . .
>
> If America is to be a great nation this must become

true. So
- let freedom ring from the prodigious hilltops of
    New Hampshire.
- Let freedom ring from the mighty mountains of
    New York.
- Let freedom ring from the heightening Alleghenies
    ˙ of Pennsylvania!

. . .

When we let freedom ring, when we let it ring from
every village and every hamlet, from every state
and every city, we will be able to speed up that day
when all of God's children, black men and white
men, Jews and Gentiles, Protestants and Catholics,
will be able to join hands and sing in the words of
the old Negro spiritual, "Free at last! free at last!
thank God Almighty, we are free at last!"

Those words will remain always in the heart, perhaps even more
than in the mind; for they are words that move to actions that reform
life.

Once I visited this Lincoln Memorial with Janusz Kukzynski,
then editor of the *Polish Philosophical Review*. As we walked
around the memorial we could see in the distance the Capital in
which the legislature sits, beside which is the Supreme Court. He
turned to me and said: "This Memorial is more important than the
Capital and the Supreme Court; Congress and the Court can make
a mistake, this building, which embodies the country's principles of
equality and justice for all, never makes a mistake."

This illustrates the way in which a tradition can bear a deep
sense of the values by which a people lives. This is not a specific
determinant of the particular decisions of a legislature or of the
rulings of the Supreme Court, but is rather that in terms of which
the people lives and strives, that according to which laws are made
and interpreted, and in the end that to which one appeals when the
system does not live up to, or keep up with, the ongoing aspirations
of a people. One could appeal to an abstract principle, but as
abstract that would leave out and be indifferent to the particular
and the concrete. One could think of this as of the past, but that
would not take account of its power in the present. The sense of

justice, as of the other virtues, is rather a living reality which transcends any particular time or instance; it inspires and rules the living action of a people simply and as a whole. This is tradition as diachronic moving through time and helping to shape the future.

For the application of this to the particular case hermeneutics, as developed by H.G. Gadamer, points to two important virtues. One is *phronesis*, the ability to adjust one's existential concerns to the circumstances. The other is *sunesis*, that is, the ability to understand the other person and to be concerned for him or her, the ability to undergo or to live with the other person or people the difficulties they are experiencing. That is not just an abstract law, but is crucial for free cooperation between persons and groups including ethnic groups in society. It is necessary if that society is to be truly personal, rather than depersonalizing.

Application then is not a subsequent or accidental addition to an ideal that is perfectly known and then applied as with techné: the notion of justice is not laid out as an architect's plans. There, when difficulties are encountered in exactly replicating the architect's plans, the builder simply omits some parts. Rather it is a matter of discerning the good of concrete persons and peoples in their complex and evolving relations to others. This is not a matter of expediency, compromise or diminishment, but rather of the more perfect concrete application of the law. Justice is realized only in the application which takes account of personal experiences and circumstances. Justice flowers and is fulfilled in its application.

Metaphysics of Interpretation and Transcendence in Being

Living through time we naturally create tradition, which is not only synchronic but diachronic. But whence the authentic newness that this requires? Hermeneutics as developed by such philosophers as Paul Ricoeur and H-.G. Gadamer points up the importance of the metaphysics which undergirds one's understanding.

Hermeneutics is basically the interpretation of texts such as the Koran or the writings of Plato, but can be as well of the traditions of a country. In Africa the tradition is not written, but oral and found in proverbs and popular stories, as well as in rituals and dances.

If tradition and cultural heritage are taken as texts , then the question is how they are to be interpreted. To read the cultural

tradition developed by a people as an object that is out there, fixed
and immobile, is to go about killing something, which, in fact, was
realized in and as life. On the other hand, can we proceed simply in
terms of the subject and ask, for example, what was going on in the
mind of a Plato when he wrote that text? This would be to try to
see with the eyes of Plato which have long been closed in death. To
see the text as a living tradition we must see it with our eyes, living
now and in our circumstances, asking our question. This brings the
text to life by developing new and creative applications for our world.
As noted above, Jaroslav Pelican has said this famously:
"Traditionalism is the dead faith of the living; tradition is the living
faith of the dead."

Our tradition can be living only if we are living; it can be
creative only if we are creative. We must approach our tradition
then, not retrospectively as something from the past to which we
must conform, but rather as a wealth of vision which is a resource
for the future we are now building.

One real difficulty in doing this is that we often think wrongly
of being. One cannot do without a sense of what it means to be; as
we live and act we operate on the basis of our understanding of
what it means to be. Unfortunately, we often think not only of our
tradition as dead; we think of everything as dead. That is, we think
in terms of a set of atoms fixed and immobile, able simply to collide
one with another as was thought by Hobbes, Descartes and their
traditions. In that case everything is a separate moment, confusing,
chaotic and conflictual. The best one can do is to join the conflict or
struggle. Some see this as the nature of the market economy or of
democracy. Indeed, it is the only way democracy or anything else
could be seen by Democritus, and the subsequent atomistic,
individualistic positivist and nominalist traditions of the first level of
freedom. But that is not the major tradition of philosophy from
Socrates, Plato and Aristotle to Gadamer and Ricoeur.

Being is not something dead, chaotic or conflictual. Being
needs to be thought of, not in its least realization, but in its highest
realization. If we experience ourselves not as mechanical robots,
but as living beings, then our notion of what it means to be real must
be primarily that of a being unfolding in time. We need to appreciate
our freedom not merely as random collection of objects, but as a
creative project unfolding the meaning of being through our time

and for our children.

Nicholas Chavchavadze was long the Director of the Institute of Philosophy of the Georgian Academy of Science. In the early 1900, his father, Ilya Chavchavadze was the founder of Georgia as an independent state, before being killed as Georgia was absorbed by Russia. Another Ilya from the same family line was, it is said, assassinated in a car collision of Georgia when he began to call for independence in the 1980s. Paul Peachey, who had visited the Soviet Union many times, when he asked where he could find thinking about the human person, was directed to Chavchavadze and his Institute of Philosophy in Tbilisi because of its tradition of work in phenomenology. The authorities, knowing that Paul was coming, sent home all the members of the Institute. Nevertheless, Prof. Chavchavadze invited him to a banquet held under trees on a hilltop where they had the fabled ritual toasts of a Georgian banquet. After the banquet as they were coming down the hill Paul received his answer. Prince Chavchavadze turned to him and said "You know, Paul, without a transcendent man is definitively a slave."

We have the principles now to see why Chavchavadze, Director of the major school of phenomenology of the USSR, would come to that conclusion. In order for our traditions to be open and creative we need an understanding of being that is open, living and creative. This sense of the transcendent, discovered in tradition as synchronic and reinforced by religion, does not leave us fixed in the way in which things were in the past, but assures that there is radical newness, new ways and new possibilities to be lived. It draws us forward into possibilities of human life which have not yet been realized. It founds life and inspires it creatively because it means that we need not merely repeat what has already been done, but that it is possible for us to do things absolutely new, never before done or even thought. It makes possible radical newness in a cultural tradition. Tradition then is not a matter of the past, but an invitation to our creativity to develop new applications; it is not retrospective but prospective.

Awareness of transcendence is developed through two types of learning. The first is horizontal learning or trial and error by which we learn how to get what we want. Primarily, this is a question of practical means which can be realized by specific human tactics to achieve specific goals. Beyond or perhaps through these many tactical moves, however, there emerges a broader and deeper sense of what life is about. We learn to distinguish between what is only temporarily distractive or temporarily satisfying, in contrast to that which fulfills or perfects in a more ample sense.

This is not remote from the experience of life. It is noted that in comparison to animals and birds humans are born quite prematurely. When born, an infant is totally dependent upon family and remains so for years. There is required on the part of others a commitment to love and care that is without preset limits and conditions. Indeed, as noted above, it is precisely by uttering such words — "in sickness or in health, for richer or poorer" — that one engages oneself in marriage from which children emerge. That is to say, human life is and must be lived in terms not of utilitarian calculation, but of open and limitless commitment that transcends anything we can define, contrast or distinguish over against others. Paradoxically, the only thing that is clear about human life is what is not distinct in terms of Descartes's notion of the components of science which are able to be distinguished and contrasted to all else.

This can be appreciated only in terms that are not fixed as formal, abstract or ideal, but of reality or being that is living, creative and loving. This is rooted in, by and as the act of creation by which we are made to be or to exist, In these terms our mind and heart is open to the transcendent by which we are and are loved, and to which we respond in love. This is what is understood as religion, and is diversely symbolized and ritualized in the various cultures and at the various stages of the emerging human consciousness.

We have here the great paradox of humanity and of philosophy, namely, that philosophy about the human person becomes dehumanizing unless we think of the human person with transcendence. That is, the human person by him- or herself or as a group is not adequately human. What distinguishes human life is its ability to transcend and live in a positive relation of love to what is beyond oneself — to others and to the absolute Other. This is the ambit of freedom. To be human is to transcend in heart and mind; to be closed in oneself is to atrophy and decay.

The notion of Chavchavadze should be extended not only to the political order, but also to tradition. In order, for a political order or tradition to be truly life-giving it needs to be lived in the open sense of being as living and transcending. This invites and urges us to move ahead in the sense of commitment to our family and to our people. It is the key to the creation of a new nation.

CHAPTER III

HERMENEUTICS AND CULTURES
(Mulla Sadra Conference, Tehran)

Hermeneutics

The issue of hermeneutics or interpretation is particularly important today as a time of great change. This is not merely a change of numbers at the end of the millennium, nor is it similar to a change of political parties within the same political system. Indeed one might even say that it is not even a change of systems, but rather a more fundamental questioning of the very significance and nature of systematization itself. In other words, it would seem to be the end of Rationalism which over the last 400 years has come to shape the modern world.

To understand the phenomenon of Rationalism it is important to return to the end of the Renaissance and the initiation of the modern period. People, and especially philosophers, had always built on their predecessors -- it was said that philosophers stood on the shoulders of their predecessors. In contrast, the modern period began with a dramatic and unaccustomed move. Francis Bacon called for the smashing of all the idols, which in fact were the bearers of the traditions. John Locke suggested that the mind be erased until it came to resemble a blank tablet.

Descartes suggested that all be put under doubt until an idea be identified which could not be doubted. The accumulated human experience was pushed aside in order to develop an aseptic laboratory in which to construct a world of simple natures and their relations. These were abstracted from time and from individuality in order to provide content which would be universal and necessary. All else was rejected as unworthy of the new modern man. Later, the fact of time would be reintroduced by Hegel and Marx, but only according to the necessary laws of the dialectic. It was a common impression of the Enlightenment and particularly of Karl Marx that religion would atrophy. What would continue would be a scientific history and only that. Thus, John Rawls would suggest that all integrating visions, including particularly those of a religious character, be put behind a veil of ignorance and kept from the public square.

It is this rationalist Cartesian world which is now being pushed aside as the radical inhumanity of the ideologies comes to be recognized. Whereas the 20th century began with high hopes for the realization of a utopia, it ends with the recognition that it has turned out instead to be the bloodiest of all centuries. Indeed Jean Baptist Vico had predicted shortly after Descartes that the new Rationalism would produce a world made up of brutes — intellectual brutes, but brutes nonetheless.

Now we are opening once again, but with renewed consciousness, to the dimensions of subjectivity and the religious dimensions of human life which had developed and been lived, but then were closed.

Samuel Huntington's now classic *Clash of Civilizations* recounts how, as a basis for identity, religion is reviving precisely where it was supposed to disappear. As young people enter upon the discovery of new intellectual horizons they experience a need for identity and for this turn to religion. Those who are more mobile, moving from village to urban circumstances, also are faced with a challenge to their identity and turn to religion as the natural foundation thereof. Thus, in the Islamic world statistics show that religion does not lessen as one approaches young adulthood, the university age, but rather, in an unaccustomed way, belief remains stable.

Huntington concludes that the position that religion is outmoded and will disappear is factually erroneous, and hence the attempts to impose a secular world view: first is false because it does not represent the broader reality, second is immoral because it imposes upon the freedom of people, and third is dangerous because the supposition that religion will atrophy does not represent the prospects for the future. These prospects are that the Western liberal, rationalist and secularly oriented peoples, who now are dominant for economic and political reasons, will soon be outnumbered as the demographics change. They will find themselves in a world in which the forces of globalization will put them into more direct contact with the larger populations of the East who are religious in their culture.

This revival of the religious basis of culture and of the realm of subjectivity as a whole suggests Heidegger's notion of a step backward as being the step forward. That is, as history moves forward humanity and especially particular cultures are faced with specific decisions. As they choose one from a number of alternate paths others paths are left unexplored and undeveloped. His example is that of Plato who chose the path of clarity, which left the dynamic elements in the philosophy of the pre-Socratics undeveloped. These, however, remain on call. Today it is possible either to move forward in relatively slow incremental steps along the path of Plato, or to reach back and retrieve that which had been left undeveloped and in that way open whole new dimensions of a meaning. This option makes possible extensive and intensive forward development. This is, of course, not a return to the past, but a retrieval from the past; what is of concern here is the degree of forward movement this retrieval makes possible.

Jaroslave Pelican distinguished between tradition as the living faith of the dead, and traditionalism as the dead faith of the living. He underlines that the turn to the tradition and to religion can be done in two different manners. Tradition is a forward oriented recuperation of the faith of the past and its development and expression in ways appropriate for the present. In contrast traditionalism is a mere repetition in the same manner of the faith lived in the past. This is often referred to as fundamentalism in relation to Christianity, Islam and other religions.

For the countries of Central Asia this is a very important distinction for they are in a very delicate position. As new countries which previously had been part of the Soviet Union they are in pressing need of articulating their distinctive national identity grounded in the Islamic faith. It is important for them to articulate this in order to distinguish themselves from the Soviet-Russian socio-political reality from which they have separated. At the same time it is necessary to do this in an ongoing and progressive manner lest they fall into a suffocating fundamentalism. They must avoid the destabilizing efforts of the fundamentalists who lurk on their southern borders. During a meeting at the Institute for Strategic Studies in Tashkent one morning in February, 1999 four car bomb explosions were felt in the immediate neighborhood in an attempt on the life of the President of the country. That evening he spoke to the country saying that that day Uzbakistan had entered a new era of its history.

Hence hermeneutics as the interpretation of the texts and

cultures of the past in the context of the present is a uniquely urgent issue for Islam. Indeed, if Islam can be read as a reform movement of the Judeo-Christian tradition the recent Iranian Islamic revolution is certainly the renewal of its religious tradition. What other challenge does it have today greater than that of making the revolution work in new times?

In this light some recent publications by the Council for Research in Values and Philosophy are especially relevant. First there is a work by Judge M.S. al-Ashmawy, former Chief Justice of the High Court of Cairo, entitled *Islam and Political Order*. Two other works by Islamic scholars are directed immediately at the issue of hermeneutics and the way in which the text lives as being and is open to human history. These are is the texts of Musa Dibadj, *The Authenticity of The Text in Hermeneutics* and Berhanettin Tatar, *Interpretation and the Problem of the Intention of the Author*. In this vein the present lecture sees hermeneutics as the living interpretation of a living text within a living tradition.

Culture

If 'to be' for living beings is 'to live', then being for conscious human beings is to live consciously and freely. Therefore to consider the human reality and realization we should follow not just the physical artifacts as would an archeologist or anthropologist, but the challenges human freedom encounters in its search for perfection through time. Here the archetype will be not matter, but rather the living God.

Value: Each being, in its contrast with non-being is oriented towards its self-realization, that is, its "perfection" in the etymological sense of "*facere*" (to make) and "perfection" ("made through and through") or complete realization. This can be striven for by many means and in many ways. Whereas animals are specified by instinct in their search for perfection, human beings with intellect and imagination are able to conceive the multiple ways in which perfection can be pursued. Their imagination works as it were as a spectroscope opening out the many possibilities and as a kaleidoscope in combining these in various ways. The great multiplicity of possibilities they uncover imposes the need to prioritize among them, giving some more weight than others. Values, etymologically, are those which weigh more on a scale in the marketplace. There is not arbitrary in the sense of creating objects, but the free determination among the real possibilities of how to pursue perfection. They relate to real, even at times desperate circumstances and the choices made therein. Values reflect the way in which a people has sought its survival and achievement; in this way their values reflect their history. Consequently peoples with a different history, for instance, one that is revolutionary such as the United States, may put special value upon self-determination vis a vis their government than do the people, e.g., of Canada who did not follow a revolutionary path.

But more concretely, in this world all things seek their being in contrast to non-being. Thus, a plant seeks to grow and come to fruition, and animals protect their sources of nourishment in order to be able to survive and thrive. Human beings also seek and strive for their perfection, but with consciousness, intelligence and imagination they are able to understand that process as one that has many possibilities; hence they are faced with choices and the need to prioritize among the various possibilities. As some possibilities are considered more important and given more weight. This is a work of human freedom because some people might, e.g., count courage as more important than harmony. So the various peoples, according to the circumstances of their history with its trials and sacrifice, set different patterns in the evaluation of the elements of their life. In this light these patterns of values which constitute a culture are in reality the cumulative freedom of a people.

A few notes about these valuations or values: First of all they are not arbitrary; we cannot survive if we live in an unreal world. But though not arbitrary, they are the result of our free determinations. In our circumstances we choose to act or not to act; we choose to act in this way or that; we find this solution acceptable and that unacceptable. All this is in the realm of human freedom.

Further, values correspond to a set of glasses. Glasses do not allow us to see what is not there, but they can shape and orient our vision. Hence, one born into a particular family and a particular culture receives a way of observing and interpreting, and a language which shapes their consciousness. In this way their values also are shaped. Consequently, we can say that values are the basic orienting factor for emotional and effective lives. We defend and act upon these values because they express our freedom and are keys to the exercise of freedom by subsequent generations.

Virtue: The other term is "virtue". If we have a particular preference such as that of harmony, if our society reinforces that preference, and if we go about learning how to live in a way which is harmonious we develop a particular capability or a particular strength in the realization and actuation of that value. But to speak of increasing "strength" is to suggest the etymological root *"virtus"* (strength).

Together values and virtues constitute an integrated vision of the way in which one can grow. This is called "a culture" — a way of cultivating our freedom personally and socially.

Further, to add to this notion of culture the element of time is to generate a tradition. This is reevaluated in each generation, because it is not there outside of us but is passed on by us. So we evaluate the content of what we receive and pass on what we find to be life giving in the circumstances in which we live and provide for our children.

What one passes on is not just history, which is all that has happened, both good and bad, but what is life-giving or cultivating. This is the nature of a cultural tradition which is both from the past and toward the future. It is learned and developed over past time as, generation after generation, people gradually reshape value judgments, develop patterns of virtues, and pass these on to their children. This is not only a feedback mechanism which as a mechanism tells us what works and what does not work and consequently shapes our behavior as a kind of Skinner box. It is also the process by which we come to learn generation after generation what is important in life, what is worth striving for. Thus, we proceed through time not only horizontally but vertically, not only developing better structures and technique but deepening as well our values and their foundations.

Tradition is also future-oriented because it is formative and because it is the consistent decision of peoples through the ages as to what is life-giving and how this can be adapted to serve as the key to life for the future. In this way tradition is not something dead and deadening, but as something that comes from life and points to the future.

Tradition then includes the two other elements: living interpretation and a living text. It implies a living interpretation because the text is read with the glasses we wear. As these glasses are developed through time then the interpretation of a sacred text, such as the Bible or the Qu'ran, or a founding declaration such as the American Declaration of Independence or the French Declaration of the Rights of Man, or of a special moment in history is gradually unfolded so that its meaning provides new insight and new values. In this way then the interpretation of the text moves through time bringing to our attention elements which are ever new and creative.

Were we to take historicity only as a movement of time and events that are randomly good or evil, there would result a relativism confusing the good and the bad. If however the history is that of an *umma* or faithful people as striving over time to live the message of the Prophet as life unfolds through time and circumstances, then tradition is better than a set oscilloscope for it interprets the text in a living and faithful manner.

This does not depart from the original text — quite the contrary! Real faithfulness to the text is an interpretation which brings out its meaning for each person in their concrete social and historical circumstances. In this way the text itself is not a dead artefact, but living as it unfolds, speaks through time, and provides wisdom which is both old and new.

Pluralism

The plurality of traditions is not a threat, but the possibility of hearing from others something which might enable one to appreciate one's own life and tradition more fully? This is not simply a matter of adding something alien to the vision that has grown integrally as my own tradition, but rather the possibility of rethinking creatively and imaginatively the content of my tradition and enabling it to speak afresh.

If the people itself is constituted of many groups, each with their own culture and subcultures, then their traditions as products of the freedom of a people are bound to be complex and pluralist. Interaction between these traditions should not compromise anyone's identity, indeed without such contact a people remains limited to the same old stories and less able to unfold its own tradition. Hence, contact with other cultures is needed.

It is important then that interchange with other traditions be neither a matter of observing them objectivity, that is, as over against us as with Sartre's "stare" nor of grafting them onto one's own culture as alien elements. Instead contact with other cultures should stimulate one's awareness of one's own culture by challenging one's assumptions and enabling one to enter deeply and to mine one's own tradition. This can be done if the contact with other views enables one imaginatively to reconfigure the elements of one's tradition.

For this, of course, a special attitude is required. This is neither a methodological sureness or defensiveness, nor a readiness to compromise by abandoning at least some of what I know to be good, nor finally the development simply of new techniques of social manipulation. Instead it is the conviction that our culture especially as religiously grounded and open to transcendence has resources of meaning that thusfar have been mined but partially, and sequently that they have more to say to us.

My own experience of studying in India made me not an Indian, but a better metaphysician with a deeper understanding of my own tradition. For over a decade I had taught the Aristotelian-Thomistic ways to God in their *a posteriori* manner, building upon the reasoning of the *Physics* and finally the *Metaphysics* to conclude at the very end of the *Metaphysics* to life divine. Encountering the advaitan philosophy of Shankara made it possible to see, however, that the "five ways" of Thomas were really saying that none of that made sense unless change was founded on the changeless as Parmenides had said it the very beginning of Greek metaphysics. I returned able to provide a much deeper and truer sense of the five ways than when I left.

A plurality of traditions, cultures and civilizations raises also the issue of possible cooperation between peoples. Cultures are keyed not simply to economics or profit in which the goods cannot be shared, but are mutually exclusive and generate competition and conflict. Nor are they simply matters of politics and power in which competition rules. Rather they must be exercised in terms of spiritual goods such as honesty and justice, harmony and friendliness which can be shared. On this basis cooperation among multiple cultures and multiple civilizations is not beyond human ingenuity.

In this light the multiple cultures and peoples appear rather according to the Biblical image of different peoples all coming with their own tradition along their own path, but converging on the Holy Mountain as the one supreme good that is both source and goal. In these terms the relation between peoples can be one not of conflict but of cooperation in a shared and hence more fully human pilgrimage.

PART II

GLOBALIZATION AS
RELATIONS BETWEEN CULTURES

CHAPTER IV

NICHOLAS OF CUSA:
AN EPISTEMOLOGY AND
METAPHYSICS FOR GLOBALIZATION
AS DIVERSITY IN UNITY
(Conference on The Philosophical Challenges and
Opportunities of Globalization, Boston)

THE EMERGENCE OF GLOBAL CONCERNS

During the 1950s and 1960s the development of technological capabilities made it possible to design vehicles with sufficient thrust and precision to be able to break the bonds of earth and soar towards the planets. By the end of the 60s, as projected by President Kennedy, Neil Armstrong landed on the moon. What he saw *there* was of little interest — a barren rocky terrain, alternating between great heat and frigid cold. But what he saw *from there* was of the greatest consequence. With a few of his predecessors in space exploration, he was able for the first time in human history to look at the Earth and see it whole. Throughout the millennia humankind had always seen fragments, piece by piece; now for the first time the earth was seen whole or globally.

At the time, astronomers sought avidly to learn about the moon. But for philosophers the questions were rather what would be found about humankind, about relations between peoples and about their presence in nature. More importantly, they wondered if this would change the way in which people understood themselves in all these regards: Would this intensify the trend to see all and everyone as an object? Or could it contribute to overcoming alienation and anomie, to transforming antipathies into bonds of friendship? But, if this were to take place, would life be reduced to a deadly stasis? Though the stakes were high, the philosophical questioning at first was languid. Now, at the end of this millennium these questions of globalization emerge with a full and fascinating force.

Why now rather than then? This would seem to relate notably to the end of the Cold War, especially if this be traced deeply to the roots of the modern outlook as a whole. At an earlier colloquium in

Manila Professor Lu Xiaohe[1] pointed out how, at the very beginnings of modern times, Giovanni Battista Vico (1668-1744) identified the limitations of the new way of thinking as bearing the potential to lead to violent opposition for lack of an adequate capability to take account of the unity of the whole. If the Cold War was the find denouement of this fatal flaw, and the world is no longer structured in a bipolar fashion, then it is no longer the parts which give sense to the whole, but the converse: the global is the basis of the meaning of its participants.

Proximately, this is a matter of communication and commercial interchange, but their full deployment depends in turn upon a politique of positive human cooperation in an integral human project. Thus today we reread Kennedy's words about bearing any burden in defence of freedom in terms of his positive context, namely, his invitation to all humankind to transcend limiting divisions and join together to make real progress. Of this his promise to break beyond a divided planet and go to the moon by the end of that decade was symbol and harbinger. The process of globalization transcends regional concerns not to deny them, but to respond to them from a more inclusive vantage point in terms of which all can have their full meaning and the opportunity to work together to determine their own destiny. This is the heart of the issue of globalization and cultural identities.

Until recently the term 'globalization' was so little used that it warranted only two lines in Webster unabridged international dictionary.[2] For the term 'global,' however, three meanings are listed:

- the first geometric, namely, a spherical shape;
- the second geographic, namely, the entire world, with the connotation of being complete. This was extended by the ancient Greeks to signify perfection itself: Parmenides spoke of the One, eternal and unchanging as being spherical.
- the third qualitative, namely, the state of being comprehensive, unified or integrated.

It is interesting to note that Webster's saw this third character of global as implying "lacking in particularizing detail" or "highly undifferentiated". Today's challenge is more complex and more rich, namely, to achieve a comprehensive vision whose integration is not at the expense of the components, but their enhancement and full appreciation.

For insight on these issues I turn to Nicholas of Cusa, born almost 600 years ago (1401-1464) at a special juncture in Western thought. Often he is described as the last of the medievals and the first of the moderns. In the high middle ages Thomas Aquinas and others had reunited the traditions of Plato and Aristotle on the basis of the Christian discovery of the special significance of existence. In this synthesis primacy was given to Aristotle whose structure for the sciences began with *Physics* as specified by multiple and changing things, whence it ascended to its culmination in the unity of the divine life at the end of the *Metaphysics*.[3] The ladder between the two constituted a richly diversified hierarchy of being

John Dewey[4] stressed — perhaps too strongly — the relation of that ancient hierarchic world view to the Ptolemaic system in which the earth is the center around which the sun and the planets revolve at a series of levels in a finite universe. He traced the development of the modern outlook to the change to the Copernican heliocentric model of an infinite but undifferentiated universe.

Nicholas of Cusa bridged the two. He continued the sense of a hierarchical differentiation of being from the minimal to the infinite, but almost a century before Copernicus (1473-1543) he saw the earth as but one of the spheres revolving around the sun.

His outlook with regard to the relations between people was equally pioneering. As Papal legate to Constantinople shortly after the takeover by the Turks — much to the shock of all Europe — Cusa returned with an outlook a characteristic of his earlier neo-Platonic training but reinforced by Islam able to see the diversity of peoples not as negating, but as promoting unity.

These broad and ranging political, scientific, philosophical and theological interests qualified him as a fully Renaissance man. In time he was made a Cardinal in Rome, where he was buried. (As a student my interest in his thought was stimulated by living for many years within 1000 yards of his tomb.) More recently, I directed the dissertation of Dr. David De Leonardis, *Ethical Implications of Unity and the Divine in Nicholas of Cusa.*[5] Expanded by the addition of sections on economic, social and religious unity, this ward was published by The Council for Research in Values and Philosophy in 1998. This paper emerges from that exploration which is summarized in the set of tables drawn from that work and appended here as figures I-VIII.

It will proceed by looking first at the manner of thinking involved and second at Cusa's reconciliation of unity and diversity in a harmony which Eastern cultures would find of special interest. On these bases, thirdly, it will look at the special dynamism with which this endows his sense of being. Fourth, it will sample briefly some of the implications which this global vision could have for contemporary problems of economic, social and religious life sketches in figures 4-7 and to be explored more extensively in the separate sessions of this conference.

GLOBAL THINKING

History

Any understanding of the work of the mind in the thought of Nicholas of Cusa must be situated in the context of the Platonic notion of participation (*mimesis* or image) whereby the many forms fundamentally are images of the one idea. For Plato, whose sense of reality was relatively passive, this meant that the many mirrored or were like (assimilated to) the one archetype or idea. Correspondingly, in knowing multiple things the mind, as it were, remembers having encountered and been impressed by, or assimilated to, the one archetypical idea which they image, all converging progressively toward a supreme One. For Cusa, with Plato, this appreciation of the one remains foundational for the knowledge of any particular. Here it is important to note how Cusa reconceives the nature of this one not solely, but also, in global terms.

To this Aristotle, whose thought began from the active processes of physical change, added a more active role for mind. This not only mirrors, but actively shapes the character, if not the content, of its knowledge. As an Aristotelian Aquinas too considered the mind to be active, but in the end the objectivity of its knowledge depended upon a passive relation to its object: beings "can by their very nature bring about a true apprehension of themselves in the human intellects which, as is said in the *Metaphysics*, is measured by things."[6]

Cusa's sense of mind unites both emphases: the original

measures the image, which in turn becomes like, or is assimilated to, the original. Sense knowledge is measured by the object; this is even part of its process of assimilation to the divine mind.[7] But as E. Cassirer[8] notes, Cusa shifts the initiative to the mind operating through the senses, imagination, reason and intellect. Rather than being simply formed by sense data, the mind actively informs the senses and conforms and configures their data in order that the mind might be assimilated to the object. Thus both "extramental objects and the human mind are measures of cognitive assimilation, that is to say, we become like the non-mental things we know, and we fashion the conceptual and judgmental tools whereby we take them into ourselves as known."[9]

But in saying this Miller seems not to have reached the key point for our concerns for global awareness — or of Cusa's, for that matter. This is not merely the classical realist distinction between what is known, which is on the part of the thing, and the way in which it is known, which reflects the mind by which the thing is known. Cusa has added two moves. First, that the One of Plato is not an ideal form, but the universe of reality (and this in the image of the Absolute One); second, that the human mind (also in the image of the divine mind) is essentially concerned with this totality of reality. In terms of this global awareness it develops all its knowledge.

Discursive Reasoning

In his study on mind,[10] Cusa distinguishes three levels of knowledge, the first two are discursive reasoning, the third is intellection. The first begins from sense knowledge of particular material objects. This is incremental as our experiences occur one by one and we begin to construct a map of the region, to use a simile of L. Wittgenstein's *Tractatus Logico-Philosophicus*.[11]

But for Cusa the knowledge of the multiple physical things by the lower powers of sensation and imagination raises the question of the unity of things which must be treated in terms of the concepts of reason and intellect.[12] For the forms in things are not the true forms, but are clouded by the changeableness of matter.[13] The exact nature of anything then is unattainable by us except in analogies and figures grounded essentially in the global sense obtained by our higher powers.[14]

But while sense knowledge is inadequate for a global vision Cusa considers innate knowledge or a separated world of ideas to be unnecessary and distractive. Hence, he concludes: (a) that sense knowledge is required; (b) that both the physical object and the mind are active in the assimilation or shaping of the mind, (c) that in this process the mind with its global matrix is superior in that it informs or shapes the work of the senses, and (d) that it is unable fully to grasp the nature of the object in itself.

As a result discursive reasoning as regards physical objects is limited in a number of ways. First it is piecemeal in that it develops only step by step, one thing at a time, in an ongoing temporal progression. Hence, on the macro level discursive reasoning can never know the entirety of reality. On the micro level it cannot comprehend any single entity completely in its nature or quality. This is true especially of the uniqueness or identity, which for humans are their personal and cultural identities.

The paradox of attempting to think globally in these terms is that as we try to form overall unities we abstract more and more from what distinguishes or characterizes free and unique persons so that the process becomes essentially depersonalizing; hence, the drama of globalization as the central phenomenon of the present change of the millennia.

In the 20th century the technological implementation of depersonalization reached such a crises that millions were crushed or exterminated — millions in pogroms, 6 million in the holocaust, 50 million in the Second World War, entire continents impoverished and exploited. In effect the limitations Cusa identifies in discursive reasoning now are simply no longer tolerable, and new modes of thinking are required in order to enable life to continue in our times.

Cusa recognizes a second type of discursive reasoning, namely, that of mathematics, which does not share the limitations noted above. But here the objects are not living beings, but mental objects of the same nature as mind. Hence the mind can pivot on itself using its own resources to construct and process concepts and to make judgements which are exact because concerned with what is not changing or material.[15] This is Humes's world of relations between ideas.[16] But as it deals only with the formal, rather than the existential, it cannot resolve human problems, but serves to exacerbate them to the degree that its mode of discursive reasoning becomes exclusive.

Intellection

Hence Nicholas of Cusa turns to a third mode of mental assimilation, which is beyond the work of discursive reason, namely, intellection. Eugene Rice contrasts the two approaches to knowledge by likening discursive reasoning to a wayfarer walking through a valley and encountering things one by one, whereas intellection is like being on a hill from which one surveys the entire valley all at once.[17] The latter view is global and the particulars are understood as component parts; each thing has its proper realty, but is also an integral constituent of the whole. It is important to note that the unity of the scene as known by intellection is constituted not by a mere assemblage of single entities juxtaposed in space or time, but by multiple participations in a unity. (Indeed, as we shall see in the next section, the multiple things in the physical order also are limited images of the whole.)

Were we to express this in terms of modern thought the distinction of analytic and synthetic modes of thought would help, but not at all suffice. With Descartes the moderns undertook a search for knowledge that was clear in the sense of identifying the simple nature of each thing, and distinct in the sense that such knowledge should be sufficient at least to be able to distinguish one type of thing from all others.[18] This gave primacy to the analytic process of distinguishing all into its component set of simple natures. The supposition was that these were finite in number, that they could all be identified clearly and distinctly by the mind, and that they could then be reassembled by equally clear and distinct links in a process of synthesis.

This has marked the modern mind and set its goals and its limitations. Having determined that only what was clear and distinct to the human mind could qualify for inclusion, due to the limitations of the human mind it was inevitable that the uniqueness of each entity would be omitted as not clear to the human mind, and that the any organic character of the whole also would be omitted, for synthesis could assemble only what was clear and distinct.

For Cusa in contrast, intellection is knowledge in terms not of the parts, but of the whole in which all participate. Here the intellect grasps the meaning and value of the whole. It works with the imagination and reason to elaborate the full range of possibilities and to grasp how the many fit together: it "depends not upon the number of things which are known, but upon the imaginative thrust of the mind" to be able to know "all the multifarious possibilities which are open to being."[19] Finally it is guided by the senses to know which of these possibilities are actual. The significance of the actual beings is not merely what we can garner by the senses, but what is known primarily in terms of the whole by the intellect.

The Aristotelians build knowledge from concrete, changing and hence limited things. Cusa's more Platonic heritage has him build knowledge rather in the global terms of the whole, and ultimately of the One of which the mind as well as things are the images. Where these were but form for Plato, for Cusa they are existents sharing in the active power of being.

The Enlightenment was so intent on knowledge that it wound up tailoring all to what it could know clearly and distinctly. As with the Procrustean bed, what did not fit these specifications was lopped off and discarded as hypothetical or merely useful. Cusa's attitude is notably different for it includes humility before reality which it recognizes, and even reveres, above all where it exceeds the human capacity for clarity of conception and power of control.

The human mind, he recognizes, has limitations at both ends of the scale of being. Even a minimal being cannot be exhaustively known. Like attempting to transform polygon into a circle by adding sides, no matter how many are added, more remain always possible; a circular shape can never be attained in this manner. Such knowledge though partial and incomplete, is valid as far as it goes, but it always can be improved upon. One can only project the circle by a thrust of the imagination.

Knowledge of the absolute, in contrast, cannot be improved upon. Moreover, it is basically unreliable for there is nothing to which the Absolute can be compared.[20] Hence, the negative way of saying what God is not and the recognition of our ignorance in that regard constitute the relevant real knowledge, for which reason Cusa entitled a major work: *On Learned Ignorance*.[21]

We have seen the limitations of knowledge constructed on the basis of multiple limited beings understood as opposed one to another. Unity constructed thereupon not only never manages to grasp such beings fully but simply discards what is not known. Thus the uniqueness of the person cannot be recognized and is lost. Conversely the unities which can be constructed of such contrasting reality remain external and antithetical so that, to the degree that it succeeds, discursive reasoning is in danger of oppressing the uniqueness of the participants. This is the classical dilemma of the one and the many; it is the particular challenge of globalization in our day and the basic reason why it is feared as a new mode of (economic) imperialism and oppression.

Cusa's suggestion of another mode of thinking whereby we think in terms of the whole is promising, indeed essential for our new age. But it faces a great test. Can it take account of diversity, and if so how can this be understood as within, rather than in opposition to, unity: Is it possible to conceive diversity as a contribution to unity, rather than as its negation?

Parmenides had shown unity to be the first characteristic of being by opposing being to non-being. In these terms each being was itself and nothing less. But such reasoning in terms of the opposition of being to non-being bespoke also contrast and opposition between beings, each of which, in being itself, was precisely not any other being. Today the global reality makes it necessary to ask whether there are more positive and relational modes of conceiving multiplicity.

A GLOBAL STRUCTURE OF UNITY AND DIVERSITY

To summarize, we have seen the new global political, cultural and economic phenomena in which we are situated and in terms of which we are called to act. In looking toward the thought of Nicholas of Cusa we saw that such a global response requires a new dimension of thinking. The characteristic modern discursive reasoning with its analytic approach of breaking all down to its minimum components and reassembling them synthetically, proposed by Descartes in his *Discourse on Method*, proceeds essentially in terms of parts rather than of the whole, of the discrete without taking account of the overall unity.

As pointed out by Dr. De Leonardis, this entails that relations between peoples and conflict resolution can be carried out only in terms of compromises which leave no one satisfied and plant the seeds of further conflicts. If now the means for conflict are so powerful as to be capable of overwhelming the means for survival, we are faced with the imperative of finding how to proceed in terms of a capacity to grasp the whole.

This pointed to Cusa's power of intellection, joined with that of the imagination, to project what we cannot clearly conceive of the individual person and the divine, to protect what we can only acknowledge of our creative freedom and that of others, and to promote the growth of which we are capable but which lies hidden in a future which is not yet.

As such knowledge is directed toward an ordered reality — ours and that of the entire globe — the central questions are not merely epistemological, but ontological and ethical, namely, what is the global whole in which we exist, and how can we act in relation to other peoples and cultures in ways that promote a collaborative realization of global community in our times?

Unity

In response to this question Cusa would begin by identifying four types or levels of unity:

1. Individual unity — the identity by which each exists as itself in contrast to others.
2. The unity of each individual being as within the whole of being. This is important in grappling with the issue of globalization in our times and is within the focus of the remainder of this chapter.
3. The unity of the universe by which the individuals together form not merely a conglomeration of single entities, as with a pile of rocks, but a unified whole which expresses the fullness of being. This may be the central contribution of Cusa's thought for a study of globalization.
4. Absolute unity — the One which, being without distinction, plurality or potentiality, is all that being can be, the fullness of being, and hence not subject to greater of lesser degree.[22]

The fourth is central and foundational for a metaphysics of the issue of globalization. Here, however, we shall focus rather on the ontology and its ethical implication. This directs our attention to the second and especially the third of Cusa's senses of unity to which the recent development of a global awareness corresponds also, namely, to the whole or total universe in which we have our being, live and intersect with nature and with others.

This has been appreciated in various ways in the past: in the totem which was the unifier for the life and universe of the primitive peoples, in the myths which united gods and nature in a genetic whole, in the One of Parmenides as the natural first step for metaphysics, and in the eschatologies and the classical hierarchies of being, to cite but a few. Now, however, after a long period of analytic and atomic thinking, under the impact of technologies which make conflict too costly and inundate us with global communications, there is special need to take up once again this sense of unity.

Contraction

The situation is delicate however, for in so doing it is imperative to avoid the kind of abstractive thinking described above in which personal uniqueness is dismissed and only the universal remains.[23]

Cusa's solution is found in the notion of contraction, that is, to begin from the significance of the whole and to recognize it in the very reality of every individual, so that the individual shares in something of the ultimate or definitive reality of the whole of being. One is not then an insignificant speck, as would be the case were I to be measured quantitatively and contrasted to the broad expanse of the globe. Rather I have the importance of the whole as it exists in and as me — and the same is true of other persons and of the parts of nature.

The import of this can be seen through comparison with other attempts to state this participation of the part in the whole. For Plato this was a repetition or imaging of the one ideal form by each being of a type. Aristotle soon ceased to employ the term participation as image (*mimesis*) because of the danger it entailed of reducing the individual to but a shadow of what was truly real. Cusa too rejected the separately existing ideas or ideal forms. Instead, what had been developed in the Christian cultures was a positive notion of existence as act[24] whereby each participant in being was made to be in itself. This is retained by Nicholas of Cusa.

But he would emphasize that the being in which this person or thing participates is the whole of being.[25] This does not mean that in a being there is anything alien to its own identity, but that the reality of each being has precisely the meaning of the whole as contracted to this unique instance. To be then is not simply to fall in some minimal way on this side of nothingness, but rather to partake of the totality of being and the meaning of the whole of being, and indeed to be a realization of the whole in this unique contraction or instance. It retains its identity, but does so in and of the whole.

De Leonardis formulates this in two principles:

- Principle of Individuality: each individual contraction uniquely imparts to each entity an inherent value which marks it as indispensable to the whole.
- Principle of Community: the contraction of being makes each thing to be everything in a contracted sense. This creates a community of beings relating all entities on an ontological level.[26]

Let us stop at this insight to explore its implications for diversity. Generally multiplicity and diversity are seen as opposed to unity: what is one is not many and vice versa; to have many beings is to imply contrast and even possible conflict. When, however, each individual is appreciated as a unique contraction of the whole, others which are distinct and different are complementary rather than contradictory; they are the missing elements toward which one aspires and which can help one grow and live more fully; they are the remainder of the whole of which I am part, which supports and promotes me, and toward whose overall good my life is directed. Taken together they enhance, rather than destroy, the unity. This, of course, is true not of the Parmenidean absolute and unlimited One which is the complete and full perfection of being, the fourth instance of unity cited above. But it is true of the third of the above unities which is precisely the reality of global unity, and the second type of unity which is its components seen precisely as members of the global whole.

Hierarchy. After the manner of the medievals Cusa saw the plurality of beings of the universe as constituting a hierarchy of being. Each being is equal in that it constituted a contraction of the whole, but not all are equally contracted. Thus an inorganic being is more contracted than a living organism, and a conscious being is less contracted than either of them. This constituted a hierarchy or gradation of beings. By thinking globally or in terms of the whole, Cusa was able to appreciate the diversity of being in a way that heightened this ordered sense of unity.

Lovejoy wrote classically of *The Great Claim of Being*[27] in which each being was situated between, and in relation to, the next lower and the next higher in the hierarchy. We have, in other words, our neighbors with whom we share, but there is always the danger that we are correspondingly distanced from other beings. Thus the sense of the human as "lord of nature" could and did turn into exploitation and depredation. Cusa's sense of beings as contractions of the whole unites each one intimately to all other realities in one's being, in one's realization, and hence in one's concerns. This converts the sense of master into that of steward for the welfare of the parts of nature which do not possess consciousness or freedom. These become the ecological concerns of humankind.

Another approach, built upon this sense of each distinct being as equal inasmuch as each participates in the whole, would image overall reality as a mosaic. But Cusa's sense of each piece also as a contraction of the whole went further by adding the importance not only of each to the whole as in a mosaic, but of the whole in and by each being. Unity then is enhanced and is the concern of each being to the full extent of its own reality understood as an integral participant in the whole.

However, both these metaphors of a chain of being and of a mosaic are static. They leave the particular or individual beings as juxtaposed externally one to the other. Neither takes account of the way in which beings interact with the others or, more deeply, are even constituted internally by these relations to others. What Cusa sees for the realm of being is relationships which are not external juxtapositions, but internal to the very make up of the individuals.

Internal Relations. This internal relationship is made possible precisely by a global sense of the whole.[28] For this Cusa may have drawn more directly from the Trinity, but this in turn is conceived through analogy to the family of which individuals are contractions, especially as this is lived as the interpersonal relations of a culture grounded in such a theology. The philosopher can look into that social life as a point of manifestation of being. Indeed, hermeneutics[29] would suggest that this constitutes not only a *locus philosophicus* whence insight can be drawn, but the prejudgments of philosophers which constitute the basic philosophical insights themselves. The critical scientific interchange of philosophy is a process of controlled adjustment and perfection of these insights.

In a family all the persons are fully members and in that sense fully of the same nature. But the father generates the son while the son proceeds from the father. Hence, while mutually constituted by the same relation of one to the other, the father and son are distinct precisely as generator and generated. Life and all that the father is and has is given from the father to the son. Correspondingly, all that the son is and has is received from the father. As giver and receiver the two are distinguished in the family precisely as the different terms of the one relation. Hence each shares in the very definition of the other: the father is father only by the son, and vice versa.

Further, generation is not a negative relation of exclusion or opposition; just the opposite — it is a positive relation of love, generosity and sharing. Hence, the unity or identity of each is via relation (the second unity), rather than opposition or negation as was the case in the first level of unity. In this way the whole that is the family is included in the definition of the father and of the son, each of whom are particular contractions of the whole.

To highlight this internal and active sense of contraction and hierarchy Cusa uses also the analogy of a seed.[30] This is able to develop and grow only by the heat of the sun, water from the clouds and nourishment from the earth. Hence each of these elements of the whole are interrelated in mutual dependence. Moreover, thereby the seed brings new being into existence — which in turn will be creative, etc. Finally, by this action of the sun and clouds, the seed and the earth as contractions of the whole, the universe itself is made fruitful and unfolds. But this is identically to perfect and fulfill the universe. Hence, the plurality of beings, far from being detrimental to the unity and perfection of the universe, is the key thereto.

Explicatio-Complicatio. Cusa speaks of this as an *explicatio* or unfolding of the perfection of being, to which corresponds the converse, namely, by folding together (*complicatio*) the various levels of being constitute the perfection of the whole. Hence, Cusa's hierarchy of being has special richness when taken in the light of his sense of a global unity. The classical hierarchy was a sequence of distinct levels of beings, each external to the other. The great gap between the multiple physical or material beings and the absolute One was filled in by an order of spiritual or angelic beings. As limited these were not the absolute, yet as spiritual they were not physical or material. This left the material or physical dimension of being out of the point of integration.

In contrast, Cusa, while continuing the overall gradation, sees it rather in terms of mutual inclusion, rather than of exclusion. Inorganic material beings do not contain the perfection of animate or conscious being, but plants include the perfections of the material as well as of life. Animals are not self-conscious or spiritual, but they do integrate material, animate and conscious perfection. Humans include all four: inorganic, animate and conscious and spiritual life.

Thus, the relation to all others through the contraction of being is intensified as beings include more levels of being in their nature. On this scale humans as material and as alive on all three levels of life, plant, animal and spirit, play a uniquely unitive and comprehensive role in the hierarchy of being. If the issue is not simple individuality by negative and exclusive contrast to others (the first level of unity), but uniqueness by positive and inclusive relation to others, then human persons and the human community are truly the nucleus of a unity that is global.

A DYNAMIC GLOBAL ORDER

Thus far we have been speaking especially in terms of existence and formal causality by which the various beings within the global reality are in specific degrees contractions of the whole. To this, however, should be added efficient and final causality by which the ordered universe of reality takes on a dynamic and even developmental character. This has a number of implications: directedness, dynamism, cohesion, complementarity and harmony.[31] Cusa's global vision is of a uniquely active universe of being.

1. *Direction to the Perfection of the Global Whole*: As contractions of the whole, finite beings are not merely products ejected by and from the universe of being, but rather are limited

expressions.of the whole. Their entire reality is a limited image of the whole from which they derive their being, without which they cannot exist, and in which they find their true end or purpose. As changing, developing, living and moving they are integral to the universe in which they find their perfection or realization and to the perfection of which they contribute by the full actuality and activity of their reality.

This cannot be simply random or chaotic, oriented equally to being and its destruction, for then nothing would survive. Rather there is in being a directedness to its realization and perfection, rather then to its contrary. A rock resists annihilation; a plant will grow if given water and nutrition; an animal will seek these out and defend itself vigorously when necessary. All this when brought into cooperative causal interaction has a direction, namely, to the perfection of the whole.

2. *Dynamic Unfolding of the Global Whole*: As an unfolding (*explicatio*) of the whole, the diverse beings (the second type of unity) are opposed neither to the whole (the third type of unity) or to the absolute One (the fourth type of unity). Rather, after the Platonic insight, all unfolds from the One and returns thereto.

To this Cusa makes an important addition. In his global vision this is not merely a matter of individual forms; beings are directed to the unity of the whole, that is, by interacting with others (unity 3). Further, this is not a matter only of external interaction between aliens. Seen in the light of reality as a whole, each being is a unique and indispensable contraction of the whole. Hence finite realities interact not merely as a multiplicity, but as an internally related and constituted community with shared and interdependent goals and powers.

3. *Cohesion and Complementarity in a Global Unity*: Every being is then related to every other in this grand community almost as parts of one body. Each depends upon the other in order to survive and by each the whole realizes its goal. But a global vision, such as that of Cusa, takes a step further, for if each part is a contraction of the whole then, as with the DNA for the individual cell, "in order for anything to be what it is it must also be in a certain sense everything which exists."[32] The other is not alien, but part of my

own definition.

From this it follows that the realization of each is required for the realization of the whole, just as each team member must perform well for the success of the whole. But in Cusa's global view the reverse is also true, namely, it is by acting with others and indeed in the service of others or for their good that one reaches one's full realization. This again is not far from the experience of the family, but tends to be lost sight of in other human and commercial relations. It is by interacting with and for others that one activates one's creative possibilities and most approximates the full realization of being. Thus, "the goal of each is to become harmoniously integrated into the whole of being and thereby to achieve the fullest development of its own unique nature."[33]

CONCLUSION: IMPLICATIONS FOR CONTEMPORARY ISSUES

There is much more to be said on these topics. The role of the imagination should be exploited to understand the nature and role of cultures. If a global outlook be evolved in which unity is promoted by diversity then the progress of world unification cannot be at the cost of the multiple cultures, but through their deployment and interaction. Strategy can move beyond the dichotomy of business and begging to the true mega project for the new millennium, namely to develop a global community in which all are looked upon with appreciation, and progress is evoked by mutual respect.

For this Cusa's global view has pervasive implications. To overcome past human tendencies to subdue and exploit nature some would want to eliminate the unique role of the humans in the hierarchy of being. Cusa would recognize the equality of all as irreducibly individual within the whole. Yet he would also recognize the unique position of humankind in that hierarchy as integrating all possible levels of the being, inorganic, living, conscious and spiritual, within the one existing being. To express that humankind realizes all the types of possibilities of life Cusa uses the term "poss-est".

This, however, is not a license to plunder and exploit the rest, but a commission and destiny to assist in bringing out of others and of the whole realizations not otherwise possible to them. It is then the view of Teilhard de Chardin[34] that it is precisely in man that we must look for further global evolution.

The relation of person to person also is shaped notably by such a vision. Generally it has been seen that order rather then conflict is the condition for the exercise of freedom. This is to appreciate the whole globally, rather than merely as a set of contrasting individuals. It is this context which truly enables and promotes the exercise of human freedom.

To see each as a contraction of the whole provides each not only with equality, but with definitive status as endowed by the significance of the whole. One cannot be instrumentalized, much less reduced either abstractly or concretely to a least common denominator. Thus equality can be promoted without the reductionism entailed by egalitarianism. At the same time, by thinking in global terms it becomes possible to see that diversity is the key to enriching the whole and thereby to drawing it closer to the fullness of perfection.

De Leonardis says this well when he concludes that

> human endeavors can be successful only to the
> extent that they achieve this integration whereby
> the isolation of the lone individual is overcome by
> social participation, and the emptiness of alienation
> is transformed by unifying love into an active and
> liberating communal existence.[35]

NOTES

1. Lu Xiaohe, "G.B. Vico and the Contemporary Civil World", in Wang Miaoyang, Yu Xuanmeng and M. Dy, *Civil Society in a Chinese Content: Chinese Philosophical Studies XV* (Washington: The Council for Research in Values and Philosophy, 1997), pp. 37-45.

2. *Webster's Third New International Dictionary of the English Language Unabridged* (Springfield, MA: Merriam, 1969).

3. XII, 71072b 26-19.

4. *Reconstruction in Philosophy* (Boston: Beacon, 1920).

5. (Washington: The Council for Research in Values and Philosophy, 1998).

6. *De Veritate*, q. 1, 8. "Truth in the intellect is measured by

things themselves," *ibid.*, I, 5.

7. Trans. D.F. Pears and B.F. McGuinnes (New York: Humanities, 1961).

8. *The Individual and the Cosmos in Renaissance Philosophy* (New York: Harper and Row, 1963).

9. *Ibid.*

10. *De Mente*, 4, p. 53 and 55.

11. *Idiota de Mente / The Layman: about Mind*, tran. and ed. Clyde Lee Miller (New York: Alaris, 1979).

12. *De Mente*, 7, p. 63.

13. *Ibid.*, p. 65.

14. *Ibid.*, p. 59.

15. *Ibid.*, p. 65.

16. *An Enquiry Concerning Human Understanding* (Chicago: Regnery, 1960), pp. 14-21.

17. Eugene Rice, "Nicholas of Cusa's Idea of Wisdom," *Traditio* 13 (1957), 358.

18. Descartes, *Discourse on Method*, 2.

19. D. De Leonardis, p. 60.

20. Henry Bett, *Nicholas of Cusa* (London: Meuthin, 1932), p. 180.

21. Trans. G. Heron (London: Routledge, Kegan, Paul, 1954).

22. G. McLean, *Plenitude and Participation: The Unity of Man in God* (Madras: University of Madras, 1978).

23. *Of Learned Ignorance.*

24. G. McLean, *Tradition, Harmony and Transcendence* (Washington: The Council for Research in Values and Philosophy, 1994), pp. 95-102.

25. *Of Learned Ignorance*, pp. 84-88.

26. De Leonardis, p. 228.

27. Arthur O. Lovejoy, *The Great Chain of Being* (New York: Harper, 1960).

28. *Of Learned Ignorance*, I, 9-10.

29. H.-G. Gadamer, *Truth and Method* (New York: Crossroads, 1975).

30. *Dato Patris Luminum* in Jasper Hopkins, *Nicholas of Cusa's Metaphors of Contraction* (Minneapolis: Banning, 1983), p. 25.

31. De Leonardis, pp. 233-236.

32. *Ibid.*, p. 235.
33. *Ibid.*, p. 236.
34. *Phenomenon of Man* (New York: Harper, 1959).
35. De Leonardis, p. 241.

PART III

RELIGION AND COOPERATION
BETWEEN PEOPLES AND CULTURES

CHAPTER V

CULTURES, RELIGIONS AND RELATIONS BETWEEN PEOPLES

INTRODUCTION

In this last decade of the 20th century we stand at a decisive point in history: a juncture at which basic human decisions must be made which, for good or ill, promise to shape the history of human kind for centuries to come.

To the Western mind this appears if one begins from the commonplace that its history of thought divides between the classical, that is, ancient and medieval, on the one hand, and the modern and the contemporary (20th century) on the other. The former is seen to have been axised upon the transcendent, the absolute or the divine. This was the One of Parmenides and Plato, the Prime Mover or Knowing on Knowing (*noesis noeseos*) of Aristotle, the "Heavenly City of Augustine or the Creator and Redeemer of Thomas. The later period, from the time of the Renaissance, has been axised upon humankind: from its early exploration of the world to the recent concerns for the human environment and from Descartes's Archimedean principle, "I am" (*sum*), to the existential and postmodern rejection of principles and foundation so that man might be free.

Present events force us to ask whether our people or any people so conceived can long perdure; and many signposts point to a negative answer. A short time ago the collapse of the totalitarian structures in Eastern Europe appeared to leave only that of the liberal, i.e., individualistic or even anarchistic, competition of the West. But the most recent signs suggest that we stand rather at the end of an era. First, the liberation of peoples in Eastern Europe, by enabling them to regain their sense of identity as peoples, suddenly has forced upon them all the unresolved issues of how they are to live together under the concrete overlapping of historical claims and counter-claims, triumphs and tragedies. Similarly, despite the narrow French vote, it is clear that any progress toward unity in Western Europe will have to give more attention to national and group identities. Second, the structures of the West seem now to have begun to crumble as well under the weight of individualistic self-centeredness. The weight of rebuilding East Germany may be the catalyst, but the disintegration seems to be rooted more deeply: wild over-consumption has generated astronomic debts within and between nations which in the last decade have mortgaged all foreseeable successive generations; moral corruption and self-seeking have undermined confidence in social structures from family to nation; the emerging sense of rights has degenerated into adversarial relations which paralyse economies, set people against their neighbors and turn ghettoes into zones of warfare and terror.

At this turn of the century there is reason to think that an entire era is passing; that we stand at a crossroads where we must choose either passively to slip further into the chaos which opens before us or creatively to open some new and deeper synthesis which assumes but transforms both the ancient thesis axised upon God and the modern antithesis axised upon man. If in the past one of these has supplanted the other, it is necessary now to think of ways to relate positively both horizons, enrich each with the strengths of the other, and open ways to make actual the sacredness of life and thereupon build the future.

There are some signs that this is now desired and sought. On the one hand, humanism no longer is taken in the closed and exclusive sense of the "scientific atheism" or reductive humanisms of the first half of this century. Disillusioned with the naive boasts that man can save himself (now revealed as a thin mask for the ancient boast in Milton's *Paradise Lost*), people search for foundations for their freedom and dignity which transcend anything that mankind, whether as individual or as party, can create — and therefore take away.

On the other hand, the churches seem to be shifting also from opposition to transforming synthesis. The "Oath Against Modernism" has slipped into the past to be replaced by the Vatican II document: "The Church in the World"; the once feared Sacred Inquisition, having become simply the Holy Office, has now become the Congregation of the Faith; in turn, the Propaganda Fidei, once charged with simply passing on what had been handed down, has now become the Office for the Evangelization of Peoples charged with finding the meaning of the Good News for the emerging sense of the unique identity of each people. This bespeaks a new sense of the foundational importance of the meeting of God and mankind in the Annunciation, the Incarnation and the Pascal and Pentecostal events which began this era.

In this light the present theme, "evangelization and culture" reflects the recent sense of the need and possibility for a new, deeper and more fruitful synthesis of the ancient and modern horizons of God and man. In our precarious situation this is a challenge to which we dare not fail to respond. How can this be done?

To begin to discern the emergence of a new synthesis we might distinguish four planes: in terms of the focus of human awareness and interests: the objective (A) and the subjective or existential (B); in terms of levels of reality: mankind (C) and God (D).

Awareness	*Reality*
A	C
Objectivity	Humankind
B	D
Subjectivity	God

This will enable our analysis to proceed in four steps. First, the present crumbling of the older Western view will be related to its limitation to the human understood in objective terms — A to C. Second, the resulting problems are seen as having pointed beyond objectivity to human subjectivity and thereby to a focus upon the nature of human creativity and upon culture as its realization — A to B (Part II). Thirdly, such phenomenological analysis in turn enables us to look more deeply into the origin of our own subjectivity and thereby to expand the focus of our awareness from humankind to the divine as the objectively transcending source in relation to which our conscious life stands as gift manifesting the intimate divine life of love — C to D (Part III). In this light, relations between religions becomes, not an alien imperial (or colonial) imposition, but the enlivening experience of being the expression of divine love, called in turn to respond creatively to present challenges — B to D (Part IV).

HUMAN LIFE AS OBJECT OF ANALYSIS AND MANIPULATION

Rationalism

In the history of philosophy brilliant new creative openings often degenerate into reductivist efforts to absorb all other meaning. This perverse dynamism is found in no less central a personage than Plato who invented Parmenides' relation of thought to being into a reduction of reality to what was clear to the human mind. Thus he invited the human mind to soar, but where it met his limits — as in taking account of concrete realities and the exercise of human freedom — he generated a classic blueprint for a suppressive communal state.

Such temptations of all-controlling reason are characteristic as well of modern times, beginning from Descartes's requirements of clarity and distinctness for the work of reason. The effect in his own philosophy was to split the human person between the extended substance or body and the nonextended substance or spirit. Much as he tried for a unity of these in the human person, this could not be done in the clear and distinct terms he required. As a result philosophers and then whole cultures proceeded according to either body or spirit as modern thought polarized between the atomism of discrete sensations and the ever greater unities perceived by spirit.

What is particularly frightening is the way in which theoretical philosophical experiments in either of these isolates were carried out by a fairly mechanical pattern of reason and then translated into public policy. It is fine for a thinker to give free range to the constructive possibilities of his or her mind by saying, as did Hobbes, e.g.: "Let's suppose that all are isolated singles in search of survival" and then see what compromises and what rules will make survival possible. Over time we have become accustomed to that game and often forget Hobbes's identification of the wolflike basic instincts by which it is played, but we should listen to others when they perceive the resulting system as predatory, brutish and mean.

Similarly, it could be helpful for a thinker to hypothesize that all is matter and then see how its laws can shed light on the process of human history. But when this was done by Marx and Lenin society began to repress the life of the spirit and term irrational everything except the scientific historicism; the freedom of individuals and of peoples was suppressed and creativity died.

Both are parallel cases of theoretical axioms becoming metaphysical totalities. It is not surprising that the result for this century was a bipolar world armed to the hilt and subsisting by a reign of mutual terror between the liberal democratic republics of the self-styled "free world" and the people's democratic republics. What is surprising is that the internal collapse of one of the partners in this deadly game should give popularity to the notion that the parallel road taken by the other partner can be followed now without fear — that the wolf has been transformed into a lamb for lack of a mirror in which to observe the effects of its own root viciousness.

Rationalism and Concepts of Freedoms

Our task, however, is not merely to identify the generic limitations of rationalism as background for the emergence of broad new sensibilities, it is also to relate this specifically to the new awareness of culture and its implications for the task of evangelization as that of the liberation of mankind in the deepest and fullest sense. Hence, we shall look specifically to the notions of freedom in order to see what the liberal rationalist perspectives do and do not make possible, and hence what precisely is the reason for the new attention to culture and the significance of this attention for evangelization.

We shall draw especially upon the work of Mortimer J. Adler and his team of The Institute for Philosophical Research which was published as *The Idea of Freedom: A Dialectical Examination of the Conceptions of Freedom.*[1] Their corporate examination of main philosophical writings identified three correlated modes in which freedom has been understood, namely, circumstantial, acquired and natural, and the corresponding modes of self (i.e., "the ability or power of the self in virtue of which freedom is possessed") namely, self-realization, self-perfection and self-determination."[2] This yields the following scheme:

Mode of Possession		*Mode of Self*[3]
1. Circumstantial	⟵————————⟶	1. Self-realization
2. Acquired	⟵————————⟶	2. Self-perfection
3. Natural	⟵————————⟶	3. Self-determination

Thus it divided three theories of freedom among three categories, namely:[4]

(A) *Circumstantial freedom of self-realization*: "To be free is to be able, under favorable circumstances, to act as one wishes for one's own individual good as one sees it";

(B) *Acquired freedom of self-perfection*: "To be free is to be able, through acquired virtue or wisdom, to will or live as one ought in conformity to the moral law or an ideal befitting human nature"; and

(C) *Natural freedom of self-determination*: "To be free is to be able, by a power inherent in human nature, to change one's own character creatively by deciding for oneself what one shall do or shall become".

When we look into the philosophical basis from which have arisen these various theories of freedom what appears striking is that each of the three types of freedom delineated by the Institute of Philosophical Research corresponds to an epistemology and metaphysics. Circumstantial freedom of self-realization is the only type of freedom recognized by many empirically oriented philosophers; acquired freedom of self-perfection is characteristic of more rational, formalist and essentialist philosophers; natural freedom of self-determination is developed by philosophers open as well to the existential dimension of being. This suggests that the metaphysical underpinnings of a philosophy control its epistemology and that especially in modern times this in turn controls its philosophical anthropology, ethics and politics. With this is mind the following review of the types of freedom will begin from their respective metaphysical and epistemological contexts and in that light proceed to its notion of freedom.

In these terms Descartes's division of the human person into a spirit or thinking substance and a body or extended substance opened two divergent paths: That of Locke bases on the physical senses to which corresponds the circumstantial freedom of self-realization and that typified by Spinoza and Kant based on the human intellect to which corresponds the acquired freedom of self-perfection. While both are important their limitations posit the way to a new level of meaning (Part II) concerned with the natural freedom of self-determination.

If the three senses or dimensions of freedom correspond to epistemologies and metaphysics, then in order to be able to achieve liberation fully by freedom of self-determination a new level of awareness would be required. When the contemporary mind proceeds beyond objective natures to become fully conscious of human subjectivity or of existence precisely as emerging in and through human self-awareness then the most profound changes begin. The old order built on objective structures and norms would no longer be adequate, structures would crumble and a new era would dawn. This is indeed the juncture at which we stand; it can be tracked on two levels. It can be read by its external signs, namely in the social upheavals and realignments of the student revolutions of '68, the minority movements of the '70s or the crumbling of the ideologies in the '80s and '90s. But really to understand these in a way that makes it possible to respond creatively, it is important to use the tools of metaphysics and epistemology in order to understand their root dynamics and to be able not simply to react, but to respond creatively.

Today the greatest peril would appear to be our blindness to the forces at work in the world and therefore our inability to provide the creativity needed to keep these from degenerating into the most base and crude forms of barbarism. Neither the liberal balance of egoistic pursuit of private interests nor the formal ideal principles of a Kantian order have proven capable of warding off colonial oppression in recent centuries and even genocide in the present decade or of channelling human forces into humane relations.

It is of the greatest urgency that we begin to chart the forces which opened the new consciousness of human existence and thereby enabled radical development at the third and basic level of human freedom at which it becomes authentic liberation. This new emergence of the sense of identity and relation on the part of individuals and peoples will be studied below.

FROM OBJECTIVITY TO SUBJECTIVITY

The Emergence of the Subject

At the beginning of this century it had appeared that the rationalist project of stating all in clear and distinct terms, whether the empirical terms of the empiricist and positivist tradition of sense knowledge or the formal and essentialist Kantian tradition of intellectual knowledge, was close to completion. Whitehead writes that at the turn of the century, when with Bertrand Russell he went to the first World Congress of Philosophy in Paris, it seemed that the work of physics was essentially completed except for some details of application. In fact, however, the very attempt to wrap up scientific rational knowledge with its most evolved tools was to manifest the radical insufficiency of the objectivist approach.

Wittgenstein would begin by writing his *Tractatus Logico-Philosophicus*[5] on the Lockean supposition that significant knowledge consisted in constructing a mental map corresponding point to point to the external world as this was open to sense experience. In such a project the spiritual power to grasp the relations between the points on this mental map, i.e., to understand, was relegated to the margin as being simply "unutterable." Wittgenstein's experience in teaching children led him to the conclusion that this empirical mental mapping was simply not what was going on in human knowledge. Consequently, in his *Blue and Brown Books*[6] and his subsequent *Philosophical Investigations*[7] Wittgenstein shifted conscious human intentionality which previously had been relegated to the periphery, to the very the center of concern. Thus, the focus of his philosophy was no longer the positivist replication of the external world but the human construction of language and worlds of meaning.[8]

A similar process was underway in the Kantian camp. There Husserl's attempt to bracket all elements in order to isolate pure essences for scientific knowledge, forced attention to the limitations of a pure essentialism and opened the way for Martin Heidegger, his collaborator and successor, to rediscover the existential and historical dimensions of reality in his *Being and Time*[9] (Not incidentally, this would be echoed in Rahner's *Spirit in the World*,[10] while the most exceptional document of Vatican II, called to draw out the religious implications of this new sensitivity, would be entitled *The Church in the World*).[11]

For Heidegger the meaning of being and of life was to be sought in its unveiling in conscious human life (*dasein*) lived through time and therefore through history. If that be the case then human consciousness would become the new focus of attention. The pursuit of this unfolding, patterning and interrelation of consciousness would open a new era of human liberation. Epistemology and metaphysics would develop in the very process of tracking the nature and direction of this process. Thus, for Heidegger's successor, Hans Georg Gadamer, the task would become that of uncovering how human persons, as emerging in the community of family, neighborhood and people, exercise their freedom in consciously creating culture, not merely as a compilation of whatever humankind does or makes, but as the fabric of human symbols and interrelations within which a human group chooses to live in the process of unveiling being in time.

To engage in the liberation of the person in our day requires examining the grounds upon which a people develops its identity as a nation and the process by which, in concert with others, it advances into the future.

This calls for attention to three specific issues:

1. the nature of values, culture and tradition;
2. the moral authority of this cultural tradition and its values for guiding our life; and
3. the active role of every generation in creatively shaping and developing tradition in response to the challenges of its times.

Culture and Cultural Traditions as Cumulative Freedom

Values: Living things survive by seeking the good or that which perfects and promotes their life. Thus a basic exercise of human freedom is to set an order of preferences among the many things that are possible. These are values in the sense that they "weigh more heavily" in making our decisions than do other possiblities. Cumulatively, they set the pattern of our actions.

Culture: Together the values, artifacts and modes of human interaction constitute an integrated pattern of human life in which the creative freedom of a people is expressed and implemented. This is called a culture.

Etymologically, the term "culture" derives from the Latin term for tilling or cultivating the land. Cicero and other Latin authors used it for the cultivation of the soul or mind (*cultura animi*), for just as even good land when left without cultivation will produce only disordered vegetation of little value, so the human spirit will not achieve its proper results unless trained.[12] This sense corresponds most closely to the Greek term for education (*paideia*) as the development of character, taste and judgment, and to the German term "formation" (*Bildung*).[13]

Here, the focus is upon the creative capacity of the human spirit: its ability to work as artist, not only in the restricted sense of producing purely aesthetic objects, but in the more involved sense of shaping all dimensions of life, material and spiritual, economic and political. The result is the whole person characterized by unity and truth, goodness and beauty, and encouraged to share fully in the meaning and value of life. The capacity to do so cannot be taught, although it may be enhanced by education. More recent phenomenological and hermeneutic inquiries suggest that, at its base, culture is a renewal, a reliving of one's own origination in an attitude of profound appreciation.[14] This may lead us beyond self and other, beyond identity and diversity, in order to comprehend both; this will be taken up below.

By attending more to its object, culture can be traced to the terms *civis*, or citizen, and civilization.[15] These reflect the need for a person to belong to a social group or community in order for the human spirit to produce its proper results. The community brings to the person the resources of the tradition, the *tradita* or past wisdom and productions of the human spirit, thereby facilitating comprehension. By enriching the mind with examples of values which have been identified in the past, it teaches and inspires one to produce something analogous. For G.F. Klemm this more objective sense of cultures is composite in character.[16] For the social sciences Tyler defined this classically as "that complex whole which includes knowledge, belief, art, morals, law, customs and any other capabilities and habits required by man as a member of society."[17]

Each particular complex or culture is specific to one people; a person who shares in this is a *civis* or citizen and belongs to a civilization. For the more restricted Greek world in which this term was developed, others (aliens) were those who did not speak the Greek tongue; they were "*barbaroi*" for their speech sounded like mere babel. Though at first this meant simply non-Greek, its negative manner of expression easily lent itself to, perhaps reflected, and certainly favored, a negative axiological connotation, which indeed soon became the primary meaning of the word `barbarian'. By reverse implication it attached to the term `civilization' an exclusivist connotation, such that the cultural identity of peoples began to imply cultural alienation between peoples. Today, as communication increases and more widely differentiated peoples enter into ever greater interaction and mutual dependence, we reap an ever more bitter harvest of this connotation. A less exclusivist sense of culture must be a priority task.

Tradition is the cumulative process of transmitting, adjusting and applying the values of a culture through time. It is at once both heritage or what is inherited or received and new creation as we pass this on in new ways. Attending to tradition taken in this active sense allows us to uncover not only the permanent and universal truths sought by Socrates, but: (a) to perceive the importance of values we receive from the tradition, and (b) to mobilize our own life project actively toward the future. We shall look more closely at each of these.

The Moral Authority of Cultural Traditions

As received, tradition is not against freedom but is rather the cumulative freedom of a people. Persons emerge from birth into a family and neighborhood from which they learn and in harmony with which they thrive. Horizontally, one learns from experience what promotes and what destroys life; accordingly one makes pragmatic adjustments. Vertically, and more importantly, one learns values, i.e. what is truly worth striving for and the pattern of social interaction in which this can be richly lived. This, rather than all that happens (history), is what is passed on (*tradita*, tradition). The importance of tradition derives from the cooperative character of both the learning by which wisdom is drawn from experience — even of failure — and of the cumulative free acts of commitment and sacrifice which have defined, defended and passed on through time the corporate life of the community.

This cultural tradition attains its authority not by the arbitrary imposition of the will of our forbears or by abstract laws, but on the basis of what has been learned from horizontal and vertical experience about life and passed on. Through history there evolves a vision of actual life which transcends time and hence can provide guidance for our life, past, present and future. The content of that vision is a set of values which point the way to mature and perfect human formation and thereby orient the life of a person. Such a vision is historical because it arises in the life of a people in time and presents an appropriate way of preserving that life through time. It is also normative because it provides the harmony and fullness which is at once classical and historical, ideal and personal, uplifting and dynamizing, in a word, liberating. For this reason it provides a basis upon which past historical ages, present options and future possibilities are judged.

Cultural Creativity and Interchange

As an active process tradition transforms what is received, lives it in a creative manner and passes it on as a leaven for the future. Taken diachronically the process of tradition as receiving and passing on does not stop with Plato's search for eternal and unchangeable ideals, with the work of *techné* in repeating exactly and exclusively a formal model or with rationalism's search for clear and distinct knowledge of immutable natures by which all might be controlled. Rather, in the application of a tradition according to the radical distinctiveness of persons and their situations tradition is continually perfected and enriched. It manifests the sense of what is just and good which we have from our past by creating in original and distinctive ways more of what justice and goodness mean. Is the reading of the tradition a matter of appreciation and conservation or of original, creative and free expression? It is impossible to read an ancient text with the long closed eyes of their author, not least because to the very degree in which that might succeed it would destroy the text which in itself was written as a vital expression of the process of life. In contrast, a hermeneutic approach would seek not to reiterate ancient times in reading ancient texts, but to recognize that we come to them from new times, with new horizons and new questions; that this enables them to speak new meaning to us; and that in so doing the texts and philosophies are living rather than dead — and therefore more true. Texts sacred and profane, read in this sense are part of living tradition in which is situated our struggle to face the problems of life and build a future worthy of those who follow.

Application of the tradition requires prudence (*phronesis*) or thoughtful reflection which enables one to discover the appropriate means for the circumstances. It must include also the virtue of sagacity (*sunesis*), that is, of understanding or concern for the other, for one can assess the situation adequately only inasmuch as one, in a sense, undergoes the situation with the affected parties. Charity or concern for others is not then alien to the progress of a culture but integral thereto.

Further, if we take time and culture seriously then we must recognize that we are situated in a particular culture and at a particular time; hence all that can be seen from this vantage point constitutes one's horizon. This would be lifeless and dead, determined rather than free, if our vantage point were to be fixed by its circumstances and closed. Hence, it is necessary to meet other minds and hearts not simply to add information incrementally, but to be challenged in our basic assumptions and enabled thereby to delve more deeply into our tradition and draw forth deeper and more pervasive truth.

A hermeneutic mode of openness does not consist in surveying texts or other peoples objectively, obeying them in a slavish and unquestioning manner or even simply juxtaposing their ideas and traditions to our own. Rather, it is directed primarily to ourselves, for our ability to listen to others is correlatively our ability to assimilate the implications of their answers for delving more deeply into the meaning of our own traditions and drawing out new and even more rich insights. In other words, it is an acknowledgement that our cultural heritage has something new to say to us and that we are the ones who can enable it to speak. This would suggest that the process of interchange between cultures is not merely one of communicating content regarding the nature of things, but of being a leaven to a culture in order that it be brought more fully to life. In this it is more existential than essential, more life than form.

Hence the attitude is not methodological sureness which

imposes its views, nor is it a mere readiness for new compromises or new techniques of social organization. Instead, it is readiness to draw out in open dialogue new meaning from our traditions. Seen in these terms our heritage of culture and values is not closed or dead, but through interchange becomes more inclusive and more rich thereby enabling life to be ever renewed.

FROM HUMANKIND TO GOD

The above phenomenological analysis points us deeply into human subjectivity and life lived in its terms. But what is its ultimate meaning? Is this new focus upon human subjectivity but another chapter in *Paradise Lost* in which humankind attempts to seize his destiny by excluding all else. Is it a new reductionism leaving humans to interact not only more consciously but to attack others more devastatingly by killing not only bodies but spirits as well. If we are newly aware of cultures is this to open new periods of persecution and cultural genocide? Very concretely, in the words of Rodney King, "Can we get along?"

To do so it is necessary to break out of our self-centeredness. We must see if the new phenomenological awareness of existence as emerging through human consciousness can help resolve the problems by carrying its analysis to the origin of our subjectivity in relation to which our love and we our selves stand as gift to giver.

The given can be approached in a phenomenological manner by reflecting carefully the mode of operation of our conscious life. One place to begin is with the person as a polyvalent unity operative on both the physical and the non-physical levels. Though the various sciences analyze distinct dimensions, the person is not a construct of independent components but an identity: the physical and the psychic are dimensions of myself and of no other. Further, this identity is not the result of my personal development, but was had by me from my beginning; it is a given for each person. Hence, while I can grow indefinitely, act endlessly, and do and make innumerable things, the growth and acts will be always my own; it is the same given or person who perdures through all the stages of his or her growth.

This givenness appears also through reflection upon one's inter-personal relations. I do not properly create these, for they are possible only if I already have received my being. Further, to open to others is a dynamism which pertains to my very nature and which I can suppress only at the price of deep psychological disturbance. Relatedness is given with one's nature and is to be received as a promise and a task; it is one's destiny. What depends upon the person is only the degree of his or her presence to others.[18]

Unfortunately, this givenness is often taken in the sense of closure associated with the terms '*datum*' or '*data*', as hypothetical or evidential. On the one hand, in the hypothetical sense a given is a stipulation agreed upon by the relevant parties as the basis for a process of argumentation: Granted X, then Y. The premises of an argument or the postulates in a mathematical demonstration are such. On the other hand, in the evidential sense, data are the direct and warranted observations of what actually is the case. In both these meanings the terms 'given' or 'data' direct the mind exclusively toward the future or consequent as one's only concern. The use of the past participle of the verb stem (*data*) closes off any search toward the past so that when one given is broken down by an analysis new givens appear. One never gets behind some hypothetical or evidential given.

This closure is done for good reason, but it leaves a second open sense of 'given' potentially important for our purpose. This is expressed by the nominative form, 'donum' or gift in contrast to the other meanings; this points back, as it were, behind itself to its source in ways similar to the historians' use of the term 'fact'. They note that a fact is not simply there; its meaning has been molded or made (*facta*) within the ongoing process of human life.[19] In this sense it points back to its origin and origination.

However, this potentially rich return to the source was blocked by the shift at the beginning of the 19th century to an anthropocentric view. In this horizon facts came to be seen especially as made by man, conceived either as an individual in the liberal tradition, or as a class in the socialist tradition — to which correspond the ideals of progress and praxis, respectively. Because what was made by man could always be remade by him,[20] this turned aside a radical search into the character of life as gift. Attention remained only upon the future understood simply in terms of man and of what man could do by either individual or social praxis.

There are reasons to suspect that this humanism is not enough for a dynamic sense of a cultural heritage and a creative sense of harmony as cooperation with others. Without underestimating how much has been accomplished in the terms of progress and praxis, the worldwide contemporary phenomenon of alienation not only between cultures but from one's own culture and people suggests that something important has been forgotten. First, by including only what is abstractively clear these approaches begin by omitting that which can be had only in self-knowledge, namely, one's self-identity and all that is most distinctive and creative in each people's heritage. Focusing only upon what is analytically clear and distinct to the mind of any and every individual renders alien the notes of personal identity, freedom and creativity, as well as integrity, wholeness and harmony. These characterize the more synthetic philosophical and religious traditions and are realized in self-knowledge, deep interpersonal bonds,[21] and under the personal guidance of a teacher or guru.[22]

Second there is the too broadly experienced danger that in concrete affairs the concern to build the future in terms only of what has been conceived clearly and by all will be transformed, wittingly and unwittingly, into oppression of self-identity and destruction of integrative cultures both as civilizations and as centers of personal cultivation. Indeed, the charges of cultural oppression and the calls for liberation from so many parts of the world raise doubt that the humanist notion of the self-given and its accompanying ideals can transcend the dynamics of power and leave room for persons, especially for those of other cultures.

Finally, were the making which is implied in the derivation of the term 'fact' from '*facere*' to be wholly reduced to 'self-making,' and were the given to become only the self-given, it might be suspected that we had stumbled finally upon what Parmenides termed "the all impossible way" of deriving what is from what is not.[23] His essential insight — shared by Hinduism, Islam and the Judeo-Christian traditions — that all is grounded in the Absolute should guard against such self-defeating, stagnating and destructive self-centeredness.

Person as Gift

It is time then to look again to the second meaning of 'given' and to follow the opening this provides toward the source as implied in the notion of gift. Above, we had noted some indications that self-identity and interpersonal relatedness are gifts (*dona*). Let us now look further into this in order to see what it suggests regarding the dynamic openness required for cooperation between persons and cultures.

First, one notes that as gift the given has an essentially gratuitous character. It is true that at times the object or service given could be paid for in cash or in kind. As indicated by the root of the term 'commercial,' however, such a transaction would be based on some merit (*mereo*) on the part of the receiver. This would destroy its nature as gift precisely because the given would not be based primarily in the freedom of the giver.

The same appears from an analysis of an exchange of presents. Presents cease to be gifts to the degree that they are given only because of the requirements of the social situation or only because of a claim implicit in what the other might have given me. Indeed, the sole way in which such presents can be redeemed as gifts is to make clear that their presentation is not something to which I merely feel obliged, but which I personally and freely want to do. As such then, a gift is based precisely upon the freedom of the giver; it is gratuitous.

There is here striking symmetry with the 'given' in the above sense of hypothesis or evidence. There, in the line of hypothetical and evidential reasoning there was a first, namely, that which is not explained, but upon which explanation is founded. Here there is also a first upon which the reality of the gift is founded and which is not to be traced to another reality. This symmetry makes what is distinctive of the gift stand out, namely, here the originating action is not traced back further precisely because it is free or gratuitous. Once again, our reflections lead us in the direction of that which is self-sufficient, absolute and transcendent as the sole adequate giver of the gift of being.

Further, as an absolute point of departure with its distinctive spontaneity and originality, the giving is non-reciprocal. To attempt to repay would be to destroy the gift as such. Indeed, there is no way in which this originating gratuity can be returned; we live in a graced condition. This appears in reflection upon one's culture. What we received from the authors of the *Vedas*, a Confucius or an

Aristotle can in no way be returned. Nor is this simply a problem of distance in time, for neither is it possible to repay the life we have received from our parents, the health received from a doctor, the wisdom from a teacher, or simply the good example which can come from any quarter at any time. The non-reciprocal character of our life is not merely that of part to whole; it is that of a gift to its source.[24]

The great traditions have insisted rightly both upon the oneness of the absolute reality and upon the lesser reality of the multiple: the multiple is not The Reality, though neither is it totally non-reality. Anselm's elaboration of the notion of privation contains a complementary clarification of the gratuitous character of beings as given or gifted. The notion of privation was developed classically by Aristotle in his analysis of change, where privation appeared at the beginning of the process as the lack of the form to be realized. He saw this as more than non-being precisely in as much as it was a lack of a good which is due to that subject. Hence, in substantial change, because the basic potential principle is prime matter to which no specific form is due, privation plays no role.

Anselm extended this notion of privation to the situation of creation in which the whole being is gifted. In this case, there is no prior subject to which something is due; hence, there is no ground or even any acceptance. Anselm expressed this radically non-reciprocal nature of the gift — its lack of prior conditions — through the notion of absolute *privation.*

It is *privation* and not merely negation, for negation simply is not and leads nowhere, whereas the gift is to be, and once given can be seen to be uniquely appropriate. It is absolute privation, however, for the foundation is not at all on the part of the recipient; rather it is entirely on the part of the source.[25] This parallels a basic insight suggested in the *Upanishads* and perhaps the basic insight for metaphysics.

> In the beginning, my dear, this world was just being (*Sat*), one only, without a second. . . . Being thought to itself: 'May I be many; may I procreate.' It produced fire. That fire thought to itself: 'May I be many; may I procreate.' It produced water. . . . That water thought to itself: 'May I be many; may I

> procreate.' It produced food. . . . That divinity
> (Being) thought to itself: 'Well, having entered into
> three divinities [fire, water, and food] by means of
> this living Self, let me develop names and forms.
> Let me make each one of them tripartite. (*Chan-
> dogya Up., 6.1-3, 12-14.*)

To what does this correspond on the part of the source? In a
certain parallel to the antinomies of Kant which show when reason
has strayed beyond its bounds, many from Plotinus to Leibniz and
beyond have sought knowledge, not only of the gift and its origin,
but of why it had to be given. The more they succeeded the less
room was left for freedom on the part of man as a given or gift.
Others attempted to understand freedom as a fall, only to find that
what was thus understood was bereft of value and meaning and
hence was of no significance to human life and its cultures. Rather,
the radical non-reciprocity of human freedom must be rooted in an
equally radical generosity on the part of its origin. No reason, either
on the part of the given or on the part of its origin, makes this gift
necessary. The freedom of man is the reflection of his derivation
from a giving that is pure generosity: man is the image of God.

In turn, on the part of the gift this implies a correspondingly
radical openness or generosity. The gift is not something which is
and then receives. It was an essential facet of Plato's response to
the problems he had elaborated in the *Parmenides* that the multiple
can exist only *as* participants of the good or one. Receiving is not
something they *do*; it is what they *are*.[26] As such they reflect at the
core of their being the reality of the generosity in which they originate.

The importance of this insight is attested from many directions. In Latin America some philosophers begin from the symbol
earth as the fruitful source of all (reflected in the Quechuan language
of the Incas as the "*Pacha Mama*"). This is their preferred context
for their sense of human life, its relations to physical nature, and the
meeting of the two in technology.[27] In this they are not without
European counterparts. The classical project of Heidegger in its
later phases shifted beyond the unconcealment of the being of things-
in-time, to Being which makes the things manifest. The *Dasein*,
structured in and as time, is able to provide Being a place of

discovery among things,[28] but it is being that maintains the initiative; its coming-to-pass or emission depends upon its own spontaneity and is for its sake. "Its `there' (the *da-* of *Dasein*) only sustains the process and guards it," so that in the openness of concealed Being beings can appear un-concealed.[29]

The African spirit, especially in its great reverence of family, community and culture — whence one derives one's life, one's ability to interpret one's world, and one's capacity to respond — seems uniquely positioned to grasp this more fully. In contrast to Aristotle's classical 'wonder,' these philosophers do not situate the person over against the object of his or her concern, reducing both to objects for detached study and manipulation. They look rather to the source whence reality is derived and are especially sensitive to its implications for the mode and manner of one's life as being essentially open, communicative, generous and sharing.

Cultural Harmony and Creative Interchange

In the light of this sense of gift, it may be possible to extend the sense of the notions of duty and harmony beyond concern for the well-being of those with whom I share and whose well-being is in a sense my own. The good is not only what contributes to my perfection: I am not the center of meaning. Rather, being is received and hence is essentially outgoing.

Seen in terms of gift, person and community manifest two principles for social dynamism in the development of a cultural tradition of harmony: complementarity which makes the formation of culture and interchange possible, and generosity which passes it along in an active process of tradition. First, as participants in the one, self-sufficient and purely spontaneous source, the many are not in principle antithetic or antipathetic one to another. Rather, as limited images they stand in a complementary relation to all other participants or images. This is reflected in the enjoyment experienced in simple companionship in which, by sharing the other's experience of being, each lives more fully: the result is more than the sum of its parts. What is true here of individual persons is true as well both of groups of peoples and of the cultures they create through self-knowledge. It is this complementarity, derived from their common origin, which makes cooperation in work and decision making, whether in commerce or in culture, fundamentally possible and ultimately desirable.

This has two important implications for our topic. Where the Greeks' focus upon their heritage had led to depreciating others as barbarians, the sense of oneself and of one's culture as radically gifted provides a basic corrective. Knowing and valuing oneself and one's culture as gifts implies more than merely reciprocating what the other does for me. It means, first, that others and their culture are to be respected simply because they too have been given or gifted by the one Transcendent source. This is an essential step which Gandhi, in calling outcasts by the name "harijans" or "children of God," urged us to take beyond the sense of pride or isolation in which we would see others in pejorative terms.

But mere respect may not be enough. The fact that I and another, my people and another, originate from, share in and proclaim the same Self, especially as Good or Bliss, implies that to the degree that our cultural traditions share the good, the relation between these integrating modes of human life is in principle one of complementarity. Hence, interchange as the effort to live this complementarity is far from being hopeless. In the pressing needs of our times only an intensification of cooperation between peoples can make available the essential and immense stores of human experience and creativity. A positive virtue of love is our real basis for hope.

A second principle for interchange is to be found in the participated — the radically given or gifted — character of one's being. As one does not first exist and then receive, but one's very existence is a received existence or gift, to attempt to give back this gift, as in an exchange of presents, would be at once hopelessly too much and too little. On the one hand, to attempt to return in strict equivalence would be too much for it is our very self that we have received as gift. On the other hand, to think merely in terms of reciprocity would be to fall essentially short of my nature as one that is given, for to make a merely equivalent return would be to remain centered upon myself where I would cleverly trap, and then entomb, the creative power of being.

Rather, looking back I can see the futility of giving back, and in this find the fundamental importance of passing on the gift in the spirit in which it has been given. One's nature as given calls for a creative generosity which reflects that of one's source. Truly appropriate generosity lies in continuing the giving through participating in one's tradition, shaping it creatively in response to the needs of the day and the discoveries of the era, and handing on this good to others. This requires a vast expansion or breaking out of oneself as the only center of one's concern. It means becoming effectively concerned with the good of others and of other groups, and for the promotion and vital growth of the next generation and those to follow.

Implications for Social Life

The implications of such generosity are broad and at times surprisingly personal. First, true openness to others cannot be based upon a depreciation of oneself or of one's own culture. Without appreciating one's worth there would be nothing to share and no way to help, nor even the possibility of taking joy in the good of the other. Further, cultural interchange enables one to see that elements of one's life, which in isolation may have seemed to be merely local customs and purely repetitive in character, are more fundamentally modes in which one lives basic and essential human values. In meeting others and other cultures, one discovers the deeper meaning in one's own everyday life.

One does more than discover, however. One recognizes that in these transcendental values of life — of truth and freedom, of love and beauty — one participates in the dynamism of one's origin and hence must share these values in turn. More exactly, one can come to realize that real reception of these transcendental gifts lies in sharing them in loving concern in order that others may realize them as well. This means passing on one's own heritage and protecting and promoting what the next generation would freely become.

Finally, that other cultures are quintessentially products of self-cultivation by other spirits as free and creative implies the need to open one's horizons beyond one's own self-concerns to the ambit of the freedom of others. This involves promoting the development of other free and creative centers and cultures which, precisely as such, are not in one's own possession or under one's own control. One lives then no longer in terms merely of oneself or of things that one can make or manage, but in terms of an interchange between free persons and peoples of different cultures. Personal responsibility is no longer merely individual decision making or for individual good. Effectively realized, the resulting interaction and mutual fecundation reaches out beyond oneself and one's own culture to reflect ever more perfectly the glory of the one source and goal of all.[30]

This calls for a truly shared effort in which all respond fully, not only to common needs, but to the particular needs of each. This broad sense of tolerance and love in a time of tension has been described by Pope John Paul II as a state in which violence cedes to peaceful transformation, and conflict to pardon and reconciliation; where power is made reasonable by persuasion, and justice finally is implemented through love.[31]

SOME IMPLICATIONS FOR THINKING ABOUT THE RELATION OF CULTURE AND RELIGION

Divine Gift and Culture

This sense of gift is of fundamental importance for the development of cultural awareness in our day. It provides the basis for understanding the basic dynamic instability of human life between limited realization and infinite openness. This engages us in the search for liberation and fulfillment from which values, virtues and ultimately cultures emerge. It situates this striving at the very center of human life. Further, it provides for an open and inclusive search for liberation in which we are concerned to share with others and grow in the very process. Finally, it provides a goal and direction for the process of liberation which elevates and transforms.

Religious vs Reductive Humanism

It is of fundamental importance to note the difference between a wisdom or overall outlook based upon humans and one that is based upon God, that is, in the above diagram between founding one's outlook upon C or upon D.

The former, focused exclusively on humans, is characteristically modern and has some epistemological roots in the modern rationalist project of Descartes to gain control over life by reducing all knowledge to only that which can be developed with clarity and distinctness. It is not that knowledge with such characteristics is not desirable, but rather that the exclusion of all other knowledge decimates the dimensions of meaning and obliterates the dimensions of freedom, creativity and love.

As seen in Part I, this begins by analyzing all into their minimum clear component natures and then relating these externally. On the physical side these components are endowed by inertia; their mode of interrelation is then that of collision and displacement. When this is taken up by those who would achieve the goal of clarity and control in terms of sense knowledge alone, as in the Hobbesian and positivist tradition, the mode of interrelation is that of power relations of self-centered atomic individuals in search of survival. The modality of such life is violence tempered only by the compromise of one's own vicious freedom. The key to directing one's life and interpreting all others is Darwin's survival of the fittest or Freud's precarious management by the ego of an aggressive *id* through a tenuous super-ego. There is in this no goal or ideal toward which we strive, but only a series of steps to curb the degree of our crassness. One not only has evolved from a brutish state, he does so reluctantly, regrets that he can no longer be simply such and returns to it to the degree possible in order to be authentically oneself.

The religious view is radically different. Its sense of reality is primarily that of the All-perfect plenitude of being. In the Greek tradition this is the One, Unchanging, Eternal of Parmenides, the Goodness itself of Plato, the All-wise One of Aristotle; in the Hindu tradition it is Brahma as the One Existence, Consciousness and Bliss; for Islam it is the One All-powerful, All-wise, All-loving; for Buddhism it is the ideal of Compassion, Harmony and Mercy. This is what it means to be, and to the degree that men are not the absolute, they are limited realizations of that Perfection, Wisdom and Love.

In this context human life does have a goal and orientation. It is not an indifferent power asking only to be able to do whatever it happens to want and to gratify whatever instinct is the most clamorous at the moment. Rather its goal is to realize its being to the fullest and to share thereby to the maximum degree possible, and according to its own nature and context, in the unity and truth, love and bliss that being most truly is.

It is not then alien or compromising for a human person to want to be with others and to be concerned for their welfare — that is natural; rather, it is being self-centered and exploitive that is alien and self-destructive. Thus, the development of a cultural consensus in the good does not do violence to one's nature and identity, but allows it to emerge and to celebrate its deepest striving. If this be the case then religious insight and outlook is truly needed and most deeply suited to human life, for it has the decisive power of the truth that responds to mankind's most fundamental striving.

Indeed, we should go further and in a way particularly related to the generation of cultures. We saw above that the development of values and virtues of which a culture is above all composed arises from the elemental instability of the human situation. As human, humans like every being has all that pertains to them according to the level of their nature. The human person is a self-conscious participant in being, and in its primary realization being is One and All-perfect. Hence, one is ever open and searching in mind and heart. One can respond to all things because one can see the good in them; one needs to respond positively to things because one can appreciate one's own imperfect level in comparison to the divine. Nevertheless, no limited reality can compel one's assent because such a reality is always deficient in comparison to the All-perfect.

This free penchant for the good is the key to the dynamism of human life. From it there emerges both the creativity and the selectivity in the life of each human group by which it makes consistent choices and shapes its culture. For this reason, religion is not alien to cultures. To the contrary as pointing out the divine origin and goal of all it gives sense to their deepest strivings, opening new levels of awareness of the implications of their choices. It opens new pathways as well for healing the human weaknesses and redeeming the human falls which stand in the way of their effort to reflect more fully and in their own way the fullness of Life of which they come and toward which they are oriented. From this follow two corollaries.

Openness to cultures. The first relates to the theme of jealousy on the part of the divine. Aristotle[32] hypothesized that if the gods were jealous they would not allow humankind to have the power of wisdom by which to see all in the context of a highest source and goal. He concluded, however, that the gods were not thus, and that such awareness was the natural culmination of the universal human desire to know. St. Paul in the Epistle to the Hebrews characteristically plunges this theme into the very process of the human struggle for liberation in terms of the exercise of its existential freedom of self-realization Paul notes that in view of the fall of humankind the Son was not jealous of his divinity but took upon himself our humanity in order that we might be redeemed by his sacrifice. He is not alien to our cultures for Christians he shares our nature and God is willing to die that we might live.

The second corollary is a better appreciation of the character of the problem which the modern search for clear and distinct scientific knowledge raises for religious insight at the present time. It is not that it necessarily denies the existence of God. Indeed, Descartes was the first to say that to do so would but weaken our understanding of the power of the intellect[33] and that a recognition of God was needed for the development of confidence in knowledge at all levels.[34] Rather the problem derives from turning the basic sensitivity of mankind from a rich sense of its reality as sharing in the divine life to instead focus upon too simple and clear a construction of all from minimal realities with no purpose other than that imposed upon it by the human will.[35] It is this clear but too simple human self-understanding which alienates man from his authentic dignity and from God, the one because of the other.

This is intensified by, and may indeed reflect, a dualistic understanding of the Fall by which some Christians see nature as corrupted and hence as absent from the divine. In this perspective, human cultures as creations of a fallen humankind can only be corrupt and opposed to authentic human welfare conceived in such a context religion could not but do violence to cultures which are seen as needing to be swept away in order to be substituted by a new creation. Catholic theology has never accepted this notion of corrupted human nature as can be seen by its DeRiccis DeNobilis and de Foncaults who reached out to Chinese Indian and Islamic cultures. But there is much to do in working out the implications of the new sensitivity to cultures for living and sharing in faith. A review of alternate models for evangelization and culture may help to make this clearer.

Alternate Models for Religion and Culture

Identification of the four dimensions in the initial schema makes it possible to identify a number of ways of looking at the relation of religion and culture.

1. If the attention to the relation of humankind (C) to God (D) is based most notably upon objectivity (A), which characterized modern thought and the earlier scholasticisms (in some distinction from Augustine) then religion is seen as a body of doctrine, unchanging in content and unaffected by human experience, which is to be passed to all cultures. Here the emphasis is on essence, nature or content. The existential condition is at best indifferent and at worst in danger of corrupting the content of religion.

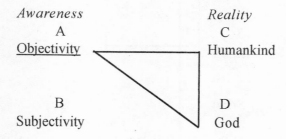

2. If the attention to the relation of humankind (C) to God (D) is based more notably upon attention to human subjectivity (B), which characterizes recent thought, then the understanding shifts rather toward the existential character of human life in community. In that case the impact of religion is a matter of transforming the culture of a people. This is less a matter of addition to, or substitution of, an alien content than of serving as leaven to the culture, favoring its fundamental realization as a search for the good, enabling it to overcome failings and falls, reinforcing once again its basic orientation to the Divine source and goal of life, and enabling it to respond in kind to the gift which it has received.

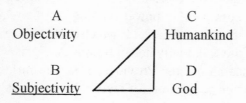

3. If the attention to the relation of humankind (C) and God (D) has both an objective (A) and a subjective (B) character, then it will be careful to keep the heritage of the faith in its fullness while seeing that this is not only expressed in contemporary modes but enriched[36] by the experience of the life of the Spirit in each people and each time. The emphasis then will be not merely upon the essential integrity of the truths of the faith, but further that these truths are lived existentially so that more of their meaning might be revealed and become part of the Christian heritage for future generations.

A   C
Objectivity   Humankind

B   D
Subjectivity   God

Issues in Need of Study

Historicity and Religion. Models 2 and 3 make it possible to take positive account of the historical reality of religion. In view of the attention to subjectivity and people's the response to religion the provenance of one's faith is of great import. This is not merely to speak of the need for intermediaries who might well be interchangeable in order that the unchanging essence of the objective content of the faith be transmitted. Instead it bespeaks the importance of Providence in the development to religious sensibilities in the various peoples at particular junctures of their history and of humankind. It bespeaks as well the importance of the pattern of the interchange of religious vision to many regions of the world.

While this relates to the patter of commercial and political interests, it is not reducible thereto. Thus model 2 is required in order to overcome political and power readings of the relation of religion and culture according to model 1, which could reduce religion to a merely human and eventually non-religious enterprise. Instead it is important to search out the Providence of God in history in order to protect it from perversion for merely human ends and to cooperate instead in the realization of its plan for the transformation of mankind after the image of God, Creator and goal of human life. Here lies much of the problem of inculturation.

Religion and the Integration of Peoples. The historical interchange of religious insight has, in fact, two directions. There is and has been a process of communities sharing their faith with distant peoples. Conversely, there is a reception of religious insight along with immigration. What mode of relation of peoples is appropriate: is it one of communicating the content of the faith possessed (A); or is it one of drawing upon their distinctive cultural and possibly even their distinctive religious experience in order to develop the faith of the resident community (B) as well? The latter is a much richer sense of the importance of culture for religious awareness.

Religion nd the Progress of Peoples. If cultures are understood as concrete community modes of realizing human life, and if this desire for perfection is ultimately a reflection of the life of divine love in enjoyment of its own goodness, then religion should not be alien to the search of communities of peoples for fulfillment, or what can be called liberation. As reminding mankind of its source and hence of the extent of the dignity and rights of all religion is thus a transforming force in the progress of peoples.

NOTES

1. (Garden City, N.Y.: Doubleday, 1958), 2 vols.
2. Adler, I, 586.
3. *Ibid.*, p. 587.
4. *Ibid.*, p. 606.
5. Tr. C.K. Ogden (London: Methuen, 1981).
6. (New York: Harper and Row).
7. Tr. G.E.M. Anscombe (Oxford: Blackwell, 1958).
8. Brian Wicker, *Culture and Theology* (London: Sheed and Ward, 1966), pp. 68-88.
9. (New York: Harper and Row, 1962).
10. (New York: Crossroads, 1979).
11. *Documents of Vatican II*, ed. W. Abbott (New York: New

Century, 1974).

12. V. Mathieu, "Cultura" in *Enciclopedia Filosofica* (Firenze: Sansoni, 1967), II, 207-210; and Raymond Williams, "Culture and Civilization", *Encyclopedia of Philosophy* (New York: Macmillan, 1967), II, 273-276, and *Culture and Society* (London, 1958).

13. Tonnelat, "Kultur" in *Civilization, le mot et l'idée* (Paris: Centre International de Synthese), II.

14. V. Mathieu, *ibid.*

15. V. Mathieu, "Civilta," *ibid.*, I, 1437-1439.

16. G.F. Klemm, *Allgemein Culturegeschicht de Menschheit* (Leipzig, 1843-52), x.

17. E.G. Tylor, *Primitive Culture* (London, 1871), VII, p. 7.

18. Maurice Nedoncelle, "Person and/or World as the Source of Religious Insight" in G. McLean, ed., *Traces of God in a Secular Culture* (New York: Alba House, 1973), pp. 187-210.

19. Kenneth L. Schmitz, *The Gift: Creation* (Milwaukee: Marquette Univ. Press, 1982), pp. 34-42. I am particularly indebted to this very thoughtful work for its suggestions. I draw here also upon my "Chinese-Western Cultural Interchange in the Future" delivered at the International Symposium on Chinese- Western Cultural Interchange in Commemoration of the 400th Anniversary of the Arrival of Matteo Ricci, S.J., in China (Taiwan: Fu Jen Univ., 1983), pp. 457-72.

20. Karl Marx, *Theses on Feuerbach*, nos. 6-8 in *F. Engels, Ludwig Feuerbach and the Outcome of Classical German Philosophy* (New York: International Publishers, 1934), pp. 82-84. Schmitz, *ibid.*

21. A. S. Cua, *Dimensions of Moral Creativity: Paradigms, Principles and Ideals* (University Park, PA: Pennsylvania State Univ. Press, 1978), chaps. III-V.

22. W. Cenkner, *The Hindu Personality in Education: Tagore, Gandhi and Aurobindo* (Delhi: South Asia Books, 1976).

23. Parmenides, *Fragment 2.*

24. Schmitz, 44-56.

25. Anselm, *Monologium*, cc. 8-9 in *Anselm of Canterbury*, eds. J. Hopkins and H. W. Richardson (Toronto: E. Mellen, 1975), I, pp. 15-18. See Schmitz, 30-34.

26. R. E. Allen, "Participation and Predication in Plato's Mid

dle Dialogues" in his *Studies in Plato's Metaphysics* (London: Routledge, Keegan Paul, 1965), pp. 43-60.

27. Juan Carlos Scannone, "Ein neuer Ansatz in der Philosophie Lateinamerikas," *Philosophisches Jahrbuch*, 89 (1982), 99-116 and "La Racionalidad Cientifico-Technologica y la Racionalidad Sapiencial de la Cultura Latino Americana," *Stromata* (1982), 155-164.

28. William J. Richardson, *Heidegger: Through Phenomenology to Thought* (The Hague: Nijhoff, 1967), pp. 532-535.

29. Joseph Kockelmans, "Thanksgiving: The Completion of Thought," in Manfred S. Frings, ed., *Heidegger and the Quest for Truth* (Chicago: Quadrangle Books, 1968), pp. 175-179.

30. Schmitz, 84-86.

31. John Paul II, "Address at Puebla," *Origins*, VIII (n. 34, 1979), I, 4 and II, 41-46.

32. *Metaphysics*, I, 2.

33. *Meditation*, I.

34. *Meditations* III-VI.

35. John Dewey, *Reconstruction in Philosophy*

36. Cardinal Karol Wojtyla, "The Task of Christian Philosophy Today," *Proceedings of the American Catholic Philosophical Association*, 53 (1979), 3-4.

CHAPTER VI

THE RELATION BETWEEN
ISLAMIC AND CHRISTIAN CULTURES
(Conference on East-West Dialogue, Bulgaria)

THE CHALLENGE OF GLOBALIZATION:
UNITY IN DIVERSITY

We come together to face a momentous issue regarding the pathways to be taken by two extensive portions of humankind in the new millennium: must they be conflictual; can they be cooperative? Our task is not to resolve that question by constructing a determining ideology, for that would destroy rather than promote the responsible freedom in which consists the special dignity — and the task — of humankind. Rather, our task is to search for understanding in depth of the present challenge, to clarify the values involved, and to envisage creatively possible collaboration between cultures.

Seen philosophically, this turn of the millenium is not a calendar numbers, a change of parties or even of systems. It is rather a basic question of how to order, and whither to direct human life. It is truly an historic juncture for civilizations and cultures. The totemic and mythic stages of the great cultures were essentially religious. This was formulated in the great religious traditions — earlier in the East, in the first millennium by Christianity and later by Islam. In the second millenium Western culture focused on human reason, beginning with the reintroduction of Aristotelian logic and its concomitant scientific capabilities. This was radicalized in the rationalism of the Enlightenment, whose denouement was the pogroms and holocausts of World War II followed by a Cold War and its threat of mutual annihilation. The millenium came to a spectacular end in the implosion of communism and the questioning of an uncontrolled market. Such a total end necessitates a new beginning. What then is to follow: which are the proper pathways into the future?

Two major formative factors stand out. The first is horizontal — namely, globalization. With the sudden end of the bipolar world system we are now in a rapid reorganization without borders. This is driven by economic opportunity grounded in the needs of a burgeoning population; it is implemented by rapidly advancing technology and communications.

The second formative factor is vertical — the opening to deeper dimensions of the human person not only to reason but to insight, not only to science but to wisdom, and not only to will but to creative freedom. Negatively this appeared in the overthrowing of the totalitarian and colonial structures which had ruled in the 1930s. At a positive philosophical level it consisted in recapturing human subjectivity through the development of existential and phenomenological insight which has made manifest the uniqueness of the exercise of freedom. Socially this has meant a renewed sense not only of the universality of human rights, but respect for the affective dimensions of human life, for the uniqueness of cultures and their religious foundations. Today there is an emerging sense of the distinctive character of cultures and of the diversity this entails among civilizations.

In this lies the present challenge, namely, how to relate both the increasing unity of globalization and the increasing appreciation of the uniqueness and diversity of peoples and cultures with their religious roots. Indeed the domination of either unity or diversity at the cost of the other would lead to a great impoverishment of human life both materially and spiritually. Economic and cultural globalization at the expense of the diversity of persons and cultures entails spiritual reduction, meaninglessness and despair in human life; diversity at the expense of effective interchange leads to physical impoverishment and cultural conflict.

COOPERATION BETWEEN RELIGIONS
AS CONVERGENT

The Divine as Context for Human Meaning

A response to this challenge must not flee the economic order of human interchange. Hegel and Marx were correct in underlining this as fundamental; any response must begin there. Globalization consists really (though by no means exclusively) in the intensification of economic interchange to unheard of degrees. Such goods, however, can be traded, but are not truly shared: what one possesses the other does not. This mutual exclusivity of physical goods is the basis for competition which, left to itself, leads to conflict. In the past, land and its resources have been the basis for wars whose outcome was the physical expropriation of the losers in favor of the victors. It is important to look for ways of cooperating on physical resources, but the willingness to do so is part of a broader set of concerns and must be inspired by higher values. It must be enabled by an imagination which is not enslaved to material goods, but capable of ordering and reordering these goods for higher human purposes.

The political is a second level and is concerned with the exercise of power. This too is a major realm of human competition. Indeed while the physical, technical and economic issues, e.g., of oil exploration and transportation, are daunting they have been soluble. It is the political concerns which raise the greatest difficulties. Here the divergent interests of peoples enter and constitute broader patterns of overall national concerns and of the international power by which these are advanced or thwarted.

Whether these can be related harmoniously depends upon the bases upon which power is exercised. If this be the economic goods involved, then political will becomes hostage to the mutually exclusive competition of expropriation and appropriation noted above. As has been said classically, politics then becomes war by other means. Hence, the challenge here is to set these political concerns in the service of peoples by developing a cooperative pattern in which all share. But if power be exercised only for power's sake, then again the result will be a pattern of dominance and subordination which can only lay the basis for economic or physical conflict or war.

To break beyond this it is necessary to reach for principles of coordination at a third level beyond the physical and the political. These must be goods which are not marked by exclusive possession as is the economic order or by competition as is the political order, but which can be shared as are the spiritual goods of the mind and heart. Knowledge, for example, can be shared without thereby being lost. Indeed, it is in discussion that ideas are cross pollinated, bear fruit and reach their full potential.

This is mirrored in the overall sequence of the work of Kant. His first Critique provided an understanding of the universal and necessary laws which rule the physical sciences. His second Critique articulated the nature of the laws which rule the exercise of freedom. Then only did he recognizes the need for a third Critique, that of aesthetic reason, in order that both might be lived in harmony. This suggests that in an analogous manner at this time of conjoined globalization (corresponding to the first Critique) and personalization (corresponding to the second Critique) — that is, of universalization and diversification — we must look for a third religious sphere in which both dimensions can be harmonized. This third awareness is not superstructure but infrastructure. It has been had by all the cultures since their totemic origins; it needs now to be brought out from behind Enlightenment hubris as the ground for creative relationships in the new millennium.

This, indeed, is the thrust of the recent encyclical of John Paul II, *Fides et Ratio*. This is an extended disquisition on the dialectic of faith in evoking reason, of reason in guiding faith, and of the synthesis of the two in inspiring and mobilizing human action. The philosophical level alone responds only speculatively to the present challenge; it would not inspire people with a living vision or mobilize them to act accordingly.

Here Muhammad Iqbal provides important orientation. Iqbal does not proceed far in his classic *Reconstruction of Religious Thought*[1] before coming to the heart of the matter, namely, that human consciousness consists of multiple levels, all of which are rooted in an awareness of the total Infinite[2] in which they find their possibility as well as their meaning.

He analyses deeply the nature of the scientific disciplines and their ability to serve humankind as instruments of our engagement in our environment. But the human issue is how people can rise above merely being a part of that order and subject to being manipulated and exploited, in order to become truly the masters of their work. He locates this in the ability of the human mind to transcend the physical order, like climbing above the trees of a forest in order to be able to see it as a whole and thereby to engage it with creative freedom. This, in turn, he bases upon the fact that the human spirit is created by, and grounded in, a total Absolute Being which frees the human person from being a slave of nature and installs one as Vice Regent of the world.

But even this awareness may not be sufficient, for it might

still be conceived in terms of possession and control. For this it would be sufficient simply to develop a system of management. But where the interests involved are so deeply human that they carry the hopes and fears of a people, much more is involved and must be addressed. Thus, Iqbal speaks of the need to recognize not only the physical and social realities and their corresponding sciences, or even philosophy as a matter of understanding. It is necessary to go beyond to the religious bases where the meaning of life, human values and personal and social commitment are anchored.

> The aspiration of religion soars higher than that of philosophy. Philosophy is an intellectual view of things; and as such, does not care to go beyond a concept which can reduce all the rich variety of experience to a system. It sees Reality from a distance as it were. Religion seeks a closer contact with Reality. The one is theory; the other is living experiences, association, intimacy. In order to achieve this intimacy thought must rise higher than itself, and find its fulfillment in an attitude of mind which religion describes as prayer — one of the last words on the lips of the Prophet of Islam.[3]

> Metaphysics is displaced by psychology, and religious life develops the ambition to come into direct contact with the ultimate reality. It is here that religion becomes a matter of personal assimilation of life and power; and the individual achieves a free personality, not by releasing himself from the fetters of the law, but by discovering the ultimate source of the law within the depths of his own consciousness.[4]

This has a threefold implication. First, religion is a matter of personal commitment on the part of persons and peoples. It engages not only their mind, but their freedom and moral sentiment, which are the great mobilizers of human action. Second, it does so in terms of the divine life expressed by such names of God as "Just" and "Loving", "Provident" and "Caring". Third, it contributes to orienting the great technical projects of our day in ways that constitute a world that is marked by these same characteristics.

Here Islam's devotion to the prophet is its unique strength. The human mind left to itself seeks clarity and control by a process of simplification. In contrast, the role of the prophet is to give voice in time to the Absolute ground of our being. It thereby reminds us that all of life, if it is to be understood and lived properly, must express in time the divine justice and love. The prophet does not leave this to surmise or indirect reasoning, but proclaims it with a voice that echoes through time — not to mention through the neighborhoods of a city such as Cairo today.

The Human as Participation in the Divine

When now we turn to the human it is crucial to retain this total response to the Absolute without which human life loses its meaning and value. In order to uncover the real meaning of human history it is essential to see how the divine as source of being and meaning is expressed in and through creation. This is a matter not merely of the beginnings of the universe, but of the creative exercise of human life through history, today and into the future.

This is the forgotten essence of the issue of peace for all humankind. Where rocks and plants just happen and animals live by instinct, humans are challenged by the need to shape their lives according to their self-understanding. In this they face a choice between three basic paths.

Forgetfulness of the Divine. The first path is to forget or to prescind from the divine ground of human life and to proceed as if humans were self-sufficient. In 1700 J.B. Vico foresaw that this emerging modern attitude would lead to a new barbarism of conflict, meaninglessness and despair which has turned the 20th century into the bloodiest century of them all. Islam has rightly rejected such "enlightenment".

For this, however, Islam has suffered a considerable, if largely unintended, penalty. According to Enlightenment theory as elaborated, e.g., by John Rawls in his *Political Liberalism,*[5] where there exist multiple integrating visions of life one draws before these a "veil of ignorance." They are simply excluded from the public sphere which is thereby constituted as a neutral forum where all can interact indifferently. From this interaction there emerge patterns of agreements regarding human interchange. These will be similar to the formal set of principles which Rawls himself worked out earlier in his *Theory of Justice*.[6] In the title, *Political Liberalism*, the word "political" opens some possibilities of adjustment of these formal patterns to particular circumstances of place and time.

In this approach, though a person may be religious in private life, as regards all public interchange the Islamic, Christian or any religious person prescinds from his or her religious vision and becomes effectively secular. This privatization of religion and secularization of public life is, of course, itself the theology described in Weber's *The Protestant Ethic and the Spirit of Capitalism*.[7] Only from that position does such a secularization of public life appear neutral, rather than neutering. This fundamentalism — unrecognized and hence unwitting in much of the West — has been the basis for the well founded suspicions that liberal values will prove corrosive to Islam and destructive of its society. Indeed, Thomas Bridges describes this as its historically inevitable derivative.[8] Religious cultures, including Moslem societies, could never accept this without ceasing to be themselves, indeed, without ceasing to be. It is essential that the West desist from desiring and expecting Islamic societies to do so.

Forgetfulness of the Human. There is a second path, opposite to the first, namely, not to exclude religion in order to proceed with the work of history, but to reject history in order to preserve the religious meaning of life. This is the path of another fundamentalism, equally as radical as the first. All that was not found at the time of a Buddha or a Christ, or explicit in the text of the Bible or other sacred scriptures is seen as contrary and unfaithful thereto. In this way, the attempt to protect the religious meaning of life contradicts the development of such human institutions as legislatures and courts by which that meaning is lived concretely.

Chief Justice Muhammad Said al-Ashmawy of Egypt has written *Islam and Political Order*[9] in order to defend such institutions from the charge of being incompatible with Islam. But perhaps more important still, a number of younger Islamic scholars from Iran and Turkey have been working on this through the hermeneutic branch of philosophy. Seyed Musa Dibadj in *The Authenticity of the Text in Hermeneutics*[10] and Burhanettin Tatar in *Interpretation and the Problem of the Intention of the Author*[11] have shown how the text and the intention of its author live through history, continue to speak in the unfolding circumstances of human life, and inspire religiously creative responses. This is to be faithful, indeed.

Participation of the Human in the Divine. The damage done by the two exclusive paths, focused respectively upon the secular to the exclusion of the religious and upon the religious to the exclusion of the human, points to a third path. This sees the human as an expression of the divine, which in turn promotes, guides and norms human development. This is the basic insight of Islamic as well as of Christian culture, not to mention the Hindu and Buddhist cultures of the East and the totemic basis of African, indeed of all, cultures. The articulation of this vision in Islamic culture I would leave to those who have lived it with devotion, but I have included a chapter on al-Ghazali in my recent work on these matters, *Ways to God*.[12]

This sense of the divine pervaded the totemic and mythic periods when all, even nature, was expressed in terms of gods. Later, at the very beginnings of Western philosophical reflection, Parmenides developed elaborately what would become the basic insight for Iqbal. Parmenides showed that to choose the path of life over death (of being over nothingness) is to see its source and goal not as a mixture of the two but as being or life itself. This transcends the world of multiple and changing things available to our senses; it is more perfect than could be appreciated in the graphic figures of the imagination which defined human thinking in its mythic stage. Thus, at the very beginning of philosophy Parmenides immediately discerned the necessity of an Absolute, Eternal, Self-sufficient Being as the creative source of all else.[13] Without this all limited beings would be radically compromised — especially human beings. It is not surprising, therefore, that Aristotle would conclude the search in his *Metaphysics* for the nature of being with a description of divine life.[14]

The issue then is not whether the notion of the divine is conciliable with human thought and life; both emerge from, and depend upon, the divine. Without that which is absolute and hence one, humans and nature would be at odds, and humankind would lack social cohesion; without that which is self-sufficient, thinking would be the same as not thinking, and being would be the same as nonbeing.

The real issue then is how effectively to open this recognition of the divine to the full range of human history. In short, there is need to enable the divine source and goal to provide the basis for the human search for meaning and to inspire a vigorous itinerary of the human heart.

To understand this Plato developed the notion of participation expressing the many as deriving their being from the One which they manifest and toward which they are oriented and directed. This operates on all levels because it is the mode of being itself. Hence, participating in the divine is not something beings do; it is what they are. The self-sufficient and infinite One or Good is that in which all things share or participate for their being and identity, truth and goodness.

This is truly a third way. It does not prescind from God — the formula of *Paradise Lost* — nor does it prescind from humankind and human history. Instead, God is affirmed in the creativity of His creation and the human is affirmed through creation by its divine source and goal. Thus, the religious basis of cultures inspires their processes of human exploration and creativity.

In sum, instead of considering the religious basis of culture to be inimicable to human progress and undertaking a futile effort at exiling it from human life, this suggests recognizing that the religious view is an essential and necessary foundation of human life and meaning. This implies searching out how this can be enabled to fulfill its task of founding truth and inspiring efforts toward the good in all aspects of life.

The Convergence of Islam and Christianity

In considering cooperation between religions it is important to note that in principle religions are not opposed but convergent. This is based both objectively, subjectively and historically.

Objectively, religions are relations to god who is one. Two Gods are an impossibility because in that case reality would be divided between them, neither would be infinite and hence neither would be God. Religions, therefore, as relations to God, are relations to the one divine source and goal of all.

Subjectively the human spirit as not limited by matter, is open to all being. Hence, it is oriented toward infinite being, which is just seem must be one. Hence, persons in exercising their religion are acting in a convergent manner. This indeed can be traced back to totemic modes of thought and followed through periods of mythic thought to systematic philosophy. My *Ways to God* traces this sequence or progression, concluding that the many ways constitute a single progression of humankind to God as it develops successive levels of human consciousness.

Historically, this relation is found between sets of religions, such as Buddhism which comes as a reform movement from Hinduism. Most striking and for our purposes most central is the sequence of the Abrahamic faiths of the Book and its sequence of Judaism, Christianity and Islam, each of which in succession can be considered a reform movement with regard to the former.

In the second Vatican Council the document *Nostra aetate* devotes a section especially to Islam, detailing the points of concrete convergence in major issues of faith.

> They worship God, who is one, living and subsistent, merciful and almighty, the Creator of heaven and earth, who has also spoken to humanity. They endeavor to submit themselves without reserve to the hidden decrees of God, just as Abraham submitted himself to God's plan, to whose faith Muslims eagerly link their own. Although not acknowledging him as God, they venerate Jesus as a prophet; his virgin Mother they also honor, and even at times devoutly invoke. Further, they await the day of judgment and the reward of God following the resurrection of the dead. For this reason they highly esteem an upright life and worship God, especially by way of prayer, alms-deeds and fasting. (*Nostra aetate*, n. 3, in *Vatican Council II*, ed. Austin Flannery [Northport, N.Y.: Costello, 1995], p. 571, n. 3.)

Moreover, the Council notes that, whereas the past history as been one of conflict, a new age and attitude is now possible and needed. Hence, it calls for collaboration rather than conflict on shared human problems.

> Over the centuries many quarrels and dissensions have arisen between Christians and Muslims. The sacred council now pleads with all to forget the past, and urges that a sincere effort be made to achieve mutual understanding for the benefit of all, let them together preserve and promote peace, liberty, social justice and moral values. (*Ibid.*, pp. 571-572.)

Indeed looking toward the future the present state of global interchange calls for such a collaborative relationship of Christianity with all religious traditions including those of South and East. But the Council highlights, the shared history and beliefs with Islam in a special way.

> In our day, when people are drawing more closely together and the bonds of friendship between different peoples are being strengthened, the church examines more carefully its relations with non-Christian religions. Ever aware of its duty to foster unity and charity among individuals, and even among nations, it reflects at the outset on what people have in common and what tends to bring them together.

> Humanity forms but one community. This is so because all stem from the one stock which God created to people the entire earth (see Acts 17:26), and so because all share a common destiny, namely God. His providence, evident goodness, and saving designs extend to all humankind (see Wis 8:1; Acts 14:17; Rom 2:6-7; 1 Tim 2:4) against the day when the elect are gathered together in the holy city which is illumined by the glow of God, and in whose splendor all peoples will walk (see Apoc 21:23 ff.).

People look to their different religions for an answer to the unsolved riddles of human existence. The problems that weigh heavily on people's hearts are the same today as in past ages. What is humanity? What is the meaning and purpose of life? What is upright behavior, and what is sinful? Where does suffering originate, and what end does it serve? How can genuine happiness be found? What happens at death? What is judgment? What reward follows death? And finally, what is the ultimate mystery, beyond human explanation, which embraces our entire existence, from which we take our origin and towards which we tend?

Throughout history to the present day, there is found among different peoples a certain awareness of a hidden power, which lies behind the course of nature and the events of human life. At times, there is present even a recognition of a supreme being or still more of a Father. This awareness and recognition results in a way of life that is imbued with a deep religious sense. The religions which are found in more advanced civilizations endeavor by way of well-defined concepts and exact language to answer these questions. Thus, in Hinduism people explore the divine mystery and express it both in the limitless riches of myth and the accurately defined insights of philosophy. They seek release from the trials of the present life by ascetical practices, profound meditation and recourse to God in confidence and love. Buddhism in its various forms testifies to the essential inadequacy of this changing world. It proposes a way of life by which people can, with confidence and trust, attain a state of perfect liberation and reach supreme illumination either through their own efforts or with divine help. So, too, other religions which are found throughout the world attempt in different ways to overcome the restlessness of people's hearts by outlining a program of life covering doctrine, moral precepts and sacred rites.

The Catholic Church rejects nothing of what is true and holy in these religions. It has a high regard for the manner of life and conduct, the precepts and doctrines which, although differing in many ways from its own teaching, nevertheless often reflect a ray of that truth which enlightens all men and women. Yet it proclaims and is in duty bound to proclaim without fail, Christ who is the way, the truth and the life (Jn 1:6). In him, in whom God reconciled all things to himself (see 2 Cor 5:18-19), people find the fullness of their religious life.

The church, therefore, urges its sons and daughters enter with prudence and charity into discussion and collaboration with members of other religions. Let Christians, while witnessing to their own faith and way of life, acknowledge, preserve and encourage the spiritual and moral truths found among non-Christians, together with their social life and culture. (*Ibid.*, pp. 569-571.)

COOPERATION BETWEEN RELIGIONS AS DIVERSE

External Cooperation

By external cooperation is meant ways in which religious cultures can cooperate in facing challenges from outside of both. Today, we have a new reality. In earlier centuries the meeting of our cultures was carried out on the frontiers where relations were often external, military, and violent. There was the long combat with Byzantium, the Crusades, the wars of the Balkans. Now commerce brings materials, notably oil, from afar and makes it an indispensable part of everyday life; the new technology of communications brings distant realities into our homes; the development of education makes them part of our growth and learning; the emerging sense of human subjectivity encourages us to interiorize these elements in our hearts and minds. We meet inescapably in every facet of our lives. Consequently, we can cooperate and we must learn to do so. But in doing so we must not destroy what is distinctive of each and thereby impoverish all, but engage what is distinctive in a shared cause. This can be done through learning from each other.

Islam with its rich sense of faithfulness to God based on its sense of His unity and primacy can contribute to the religious life of the West what is most essential, namely, the sense of God.

In return, the Church in the West has struggled for many centuries with the threats that Islam most fears, namely, reductivism, rationalism and materialism. It has learned by its failures as well as its successes how to live religiously in a culture that is distracted by possessions and inundated by images. These are projected by techniques drawn from sophisticated psychological research and generally are at the service of commercial and ideological interests, often contrary to religion. It could be expected that Christianity which has grown with these challenges in the West might have insights which could be helpful in protecting and promoting religious life in Islam in these times of change.

To recount these lessons would be a long study in its own right. They would include the need to distinguish the multiple orders of human awareness and to locate that which is proper to the religious; the process of relating religion in each of these modes with the levels of theoretical and practical consciousness to the mutual benefit of both; and not least the Vatican II document on religious liberty affirming as a modern accomplishment the need to recognize the rights of conscience of every person with regard to his or her religious belief — this it considered less a deductive than an inductive insight drawn from human experience.

In his book, *Seize the Moment*,[15] Richard Nixon suggests a principle for such mutual Islamic-Christian exchange, namely, that it is not one's business to determine what others will be or do, but only to help them become what they will to be. This reflects well the new sense of the person and the new respect for the interiority of the spirit and hence for human freedom. It echoes the classical sense of the love of benevolence in which the good is willed for the other without seeking what it will do for us. We have all experienced this in our families where we came first to experience God's creative benevolence in our lives.

This is the suggestion of Vatican II, namely, that we have much to share and the ability to cooperate in facing challenges from outside of both Christianity and Islam, e.g., in safeguarding and fostering social justice and moral virtues. It is essential for religions to cooperate creatively in developing for the next millenium a broader world civilization which prospers through productive interchange, shared benevolence and peace.

Internal Cooperation

There is also need for internal cooperation, that is, in helping one another not only to be able effectively to withstand contemporary challenges but even to draw more richly on its own resource.

In the introduction the challenge was stated to consist not only in globalization in which one reaches out to others and discovers points of convergent principle or experience, but in personalization in which there emerges a greater consciousness of the differences between peoples. Were dialogue and cooperation to result only from the ways we are the same then the road to peace would lie in suppressing that which is distinctive of persons and their cultures or rendering it inoperative in the public square. This has been a strong factor in the liberal "approach". If, instead, personal life is appreciated as creative and hence as differentiating the pattern of one's life and culture, then it is necessary to find ways in which even the differences in human and cultural formation can be principles of cooperation, indeed even a means for the internal enrichment of traditions from their proper resources. Only this will make it possible truly to turn swords into ploughshares for the tasks of new millennium.

To understand how this can be so it is necessary first to see how cultures are constituted of the cumulative exercise of that human freedom. If for a living being "to be is to live," then for a human being "to be is to live consciously, creatively and responsibly". Inevitably this creates the uniqueness and hence the diversity of our lives as we respond to different physical and social challenges with distinctive resources, each in our own manner. Further as this is identically to live out our participation in the divine which is the essence of religion, we can expect that not only our cultures will be diverse, but also the religious roots of these cultures.

As seen above, relation to the divine as shared by all peoples provides the basis for cooperation between the many peoples in their efforts at development. But, this is not a matter of theory separated from life or of practice separated from vision. It is, in fact, the wisdom core of the distinctive cultural tradition into which we are born and though which we interpret and respond to the challenges of development in cooperation with others in an ever more inconnected world.

In order then to look for the bases of peace in the process of development we must search not only for possible convergences of interests, but at the distinctive cultural contexts in terms of which these interests are defined; we must look also for the possibility of one culture contributing to the internal and self-consistent growth of another. This entails three issues: the uniqueness of cultural traditions; their roots in the religious commitment of each people; and the way in which people's with diverse cultural and religious commitments can contribute positively one to another not only through that in which they concur, as was noted above, but also through their cultural divergences.

The Distinctness of Cultural Traditions

Culture. A culture can be understood as that complex of values and virtues by which a people lives. The term 'value' was derived from the economic sphere where it meant the amount of a commodity required in order to bring a certain price. This is reflected also in the term 'axiology,' the root of which means "weighing as much" or "worth as much." This has objective content, for the good must really "weigh in" — it must make a real difference.[16]

'Value' expresses this good especially as related to persons who actually acknowledge it as a good and respond to it as desirable. Thus, different individuals or groups, or possibly the same group but at different periods, may have distinct sets of values as they become sensitive to, and prize alternate sets of goods. More generally, over time a subtle shift takes place in the distinctive ranking of the degree to which various goods are prized.

By so doing among objective moral goods a certain pattern of values is delineated which in a more stable fashion mirrors the corporate free choices of a people. Further, the exercise of these choices develops special capabilities or virtues as it is in these ways of acting and reacting that we are practiced. These capabilities constitute the basic topology of a culture; as repeatedly reaffirmed through time, they build a tradition or heritage.

By giving shape to the culture, values and virtues constitute the prime pattern and gradation of goods experienced from their earliest years by persons born into that heritage. In these terms they interpret and shape the development of their relations with other persons and groups. Thus, young persons, as it were, peer out at the world through cultural lenses which were formed by their family and ancestors and which reflect the pattern of choices made by their community through its long history — often in its most trying circumstances. Like a pair of glasses, values do not create the object, but reveal and focus attention upon certain goods and patterns of goods, rather than upon others.

In this way values and virtues become the basic orienting factor for one's intellectual, affective and emotional life. Over time, they encourage certain patterns of action — and even of physical growth — which, in turn, reinforce the pattern of values and virtues. Through this process we constitute our universe of moral concern in which we struggle to achieve, mourn our failures, and celebrate our successes. This is our world of hopes and fears in terms of which, as Plato wrote in the *Laches*, our lives have moral meaning[17] and we can speak properly of values. It is of this that the Prophet speaks the words of God.

Cultural Traditions. To relate culture to tradition John Caputo, in *Philosophical Foundations for Moral Education and Character Development*,[18] notes that from the very beginning one's life is lived with others. Even before birth, one's consciousness emerges as awareness of the biological rhythms of one's mother which reflect, in turn, her peace or fears. Upon birth there follows a progressively broader sharing in the life of parents and siblings. In this context one is fully at peace, and hence most open to personal growth and social development. Hence, from its beginning one's life is social and historical: One learns from one's family which through time depends upon earlier generations. This is the universal condition of each person, and consequently of the development of human aware ness and of knowledge.

Interpersonal dependence is then not unnatural — quite the contrary, we depend for our being upon our creator, we are conceived in dependence upon our parents, and we are nurtured by them with care and concern. Through the years we depend continually upon our family and peers, school and community.

We turn to other persons whom we recognize as superior in terms not of their will, but of their insight and judgment — and precisely in those matters where truth, reason and balanced judgment are required. The preeminence or authority of wise persons in the community is not something they usurp or with which they are arbitrarily endowed. It is based upon their capabilities and acknowledged in our free and reasoned response. Thus, the burden of Plato's *Republic* is precisely the education of the future leader to be able to exercise authority.

From this notion of authority in a cultural community it is possible to construct that of tradition by taking account of the preceding generations with their accumulation of human insight predicated upon the wealth of their human experience through time. As a process of trial and error, of continual correction and addition, history constitutes a type of learning and testing laboratory in which the strengths of various insights can be identified and reinforced, while their deficiencies are corrected and complemented. We learn from experience what promotes and what destroys life, and accordingly we make pragmatic adjustments. The cumulative results of this extended process of learning and testing constitute tradition.

But even this language remains too abstract, too limited to method or technique, too unidimensional. While tradition can be described in terms of feed-back mechanisms and might seem merely to concern how to cope in daily life, what is being spoken about are free acts. These express passionate human commitment and personal sacrifice in responding to concrete dangers, building and rebuilding family alliances, and constructing and defending one's nation.

Moreover, this wisdom is not a matter of mere tactical adjustments to temporary concerns. It concerns rather the meaning we are able to envision for life and which we desire to achieve through all such adjustments over a period of generations: it is what is truly worth striving for.

This points us beyond the horizontal plane of the various ages of history and directs our attention vertically to its ground and, hence, to the religious bases of the values we seek to realize in concrete circumstances. The history of Abraham, our common father in faith, is a concrete account of the process through history of deep wisdom in interaction with the divine.

The content of a tradition serves as a model and exemplar, not because of personal inertia, but because of the corporate character of learning. This was built out of experience consisting of the free and wise acts of the successive generations of a people in reevaluating, reaffirming, preserving and passing on what has been learned. The content of any long tradition has passed the test of countless generations. Standing, as it were, on the shoulders of our forebears, those who come later are able to discover possibilities and evaluate situations with the help of their vision of the elders because of the sensitivity they developed and communicated to us. Without this we could not even choose the topics to be investigated or awaken within ourselves the desire to study those problems.

Cultural traditions, then, are not simply everything that ever happened, but only what has appeared significant to a particular distinctive people, been judged as life giving, and actively transmitted to their next generation. It is by definition then the good as humanely appreciated by a people; its presentation by different voices draws out its many aspects. Thus a cultural tradition is not an object in itself, but a rich and flowing river from which multiple themes can be drawn according to the motivation and interest of the inquirer. It needs to be accepted and embraced, affirmed and cultivated. Here the emphasis is neither upon the past or the present, but upon a people living through time.

Tradition is not a passive storehouse of materials to be drawn upon and shaped at the arbitrary will of the present inquirer. Rather, it presents insight and wisdom that is normative for life in the present and future, for its harmony of measure and fullness suggest a way for the mature and perfect formation of the members of this people.[19] Such a vision is both historical and normative: historical, because arising in time and presenting the characteristic manner in which a people preserves and promotes human life through time; and normative, because presenting a basis upon which to judge past ages, to guide present actions and to choose among options for the future. The fact of human striving manifests that every humanism, far from being indifferent, is committed to the realization of some such classical and perduring model of perfection.

Relations between Religious Cultures

The danger, of course, and one that is foundational is whether the combination of the deep immersion in, and commitment to, one's cultural tradition thereby traps one in insuperable opposition to the interests and strivings of those in other traditions. Can we overcome such opposition? Indeed can the commitments others have to their own cultural tradition become a means for us to look into our own traditions — and vice versa? If so, this would provide the key to effective cooperation between religious and cultures.

It should be understood that cultural traditions will be multiple according to the historical grouping of people, the diverse circumstances in which they shape their lives and the specific challenges to which they respond and in so doing ever more profoundly shape themselves. More foundationally they reflect the specific mode in which God chooses to speak to his peoples and the message he conveys through his prophets to help peoples find their way on their pilgrimages.

Contemporary attention to the person enables us to be more conscious of the distinctive formative pattern of our proper culture and its religious foundations. This can enable us to appreciate it as uniquely different among others. However, being situated among one's own people and hearing the same stories told in the same way, one's appreciation of the rich content of one's tradition could remain limited.

The way to break out of this limitation of the human condition is to encounter other peoples with other experiences in order to check one's bearings. This is not to copy the other or to graft alien elements onto one's culture. It is rather to be stimulated by the experience of others and thus enabled to go more deeply into one's own cultural heritage and sacred books. Here the aim is to draw out meaning which had always been there in the Infinite ground of my culture, but which thusfar had not been sounded.

Rather than abandoning or lessening allegiance to one's cultural tradition this is a higher fidelity thereto. It is built on the conviction that my tradition as grounded in the infinite divine is richer than I or my people have thus far been able to sound, that it has more to say to us, and hence that we need to be open to new dimensions of its meaning.

This is the special opportunity of our time of globalization, communication and mutual interaction. Rather than looking upon the other as a threat, communication with other cultures as they plum their own religious tradition can enable one to draw more fully upon one's own. This enables one to cooperate with others in the development of their own cultures from the resources of their own religious tradition. In this way all religious cultures are promoted, each in their unique character. This is more than a dialogue between differences; it is cooperation in developing distinct but convergent pathways for the coming millenium.

NOTES

1. Muhammad Iqbal, *The Reconstruction of Religious Thought*, ed. Saeed Sheikh (Lahore: Iqbal Academy of Pakistan and the Institute of Islamic Culture, 1986).

2. *Ibid.*, p. 4-5.

3. *Ibid.*, p. 49.

4. *Ibid.*, p. 143.

5. (New York: Columbia University Press, 1993).

6. (Cambridge, Mass.: Belknap, 1971).

7. (Washington: The Council for Research in Values and Philosophy, 1994).

8 (Washington: The Council for Research in Values and Philosophy, 1998).

9. *The Culture of Citizenship, Inventing Postmodern Civil Culture* (Albany: State University of New York Press, 1990), chap. I.

10. (Washington: The Council for Research in Values and Philosophy, 1998).

11. (Washington: The Council for Research in Values and Philosophy, 1999).

12. (Washington: The Council for Research in Values and Philosophy, 1999).

13. Parmenides, Fragment 8, see McLean and Aspell,

Readings on Ancient Western Philosophy (Englewood Cliffs, NY: Prentice Hall, 1990).

14. Fragments in G.F. McLean and P. Aspell, *Readings in Ancient Western Philosophy* (Englewood Cliffs, NJ.: Prentice Hall, 1971), pp. 39-44. Neither being nor thought makes sense if being is the same as nonbeing, for then to do, say or be anything would be the same as not doing, not saying or not being. But the real must be irreducible to nothing and being to nonbeing if there is any thing or any meaning whatsoever. Hence being must have about it the self-sufficiency expressed by Parmenides's notion of the absolute One.

15. Richard Nixon, *Seize the Moment* (New York: Simon & Schuster, c1992).

16. Ivor Leclerc, "The Metaphysics of the Good," *Review of Metaphysics*, 35 (1981), 3-5. See also *Vocabulaire technique et critique de la philosophie*, ed. André Lalande (Paris: PUF, 1956), pp. 1182-1186.

17. J. Mehta, *Martin Heidegger: The Way and the Vision* (Honolulu: Univ. of Hawaii Press, 1967), pp. 90-91.

18. R. Carnap, *Vienna Manifesto*, trans. A. Blumberg in G. Kreyche and J. Mann, *Perspectives on Reality* (New York: Harcourt, Brace and World, 1966), p. 485.

19. H.G. Gadamer, *Truth and Method* (New York: Crossroads, 1975), pp. 240, 246-247, 305-310.

CHAPTER VII

ISLAM AS SEEN FROM
THE CHRISTIAN WEST
(Al-Azhar University, Cairo)

The question of how Islam is seen from the West is especially difficult because both Islam and the West are vast and complex. Islam constitutes an integrated way of life which includes all aspects from personal piety, through family life to society. The West in contrast is relatively disaggregated including a broad range of attitudes to life ranging from a materialistic consumerism to a deeply religious sense of person and community.

With such a large number of aspects and possible viewpoints any attempt to select a few from either side and relate these to a few from the other would be arbitrary, limited, and thereby inadequate — if not even deceptive and downright dangerous.

However, a recent work by David Gress, *From Plato to NATO: The Idea of the West and Its Opponents* suggests that the West should be understood not in terms of the Greeks, but in terms of the high middle ages when Greek philosophy and political theory was reintegrated into the Christian West; this began with the Christianization of the Roman empire in the fourth century AD. This would then be characterized by Christian morality, Germanic heroic freedom and classical Greek virtue. (He further contrasts this "old West" to the "new West" of democracy, capitalism and science.) In this light the relation of Islam to the West comes into greater focus as the relation of the two integrating religious cultures: Islam and Christianity.

PERSON AND RELIGION

Hence, a more helpful and interesting approach may be to look to some basic integrating themes such as person, society and culture which have been emerging throughout the world and to see how these are perceived in the two cultures. In the last 50 years the general flow of human aspirations and events has brought to the fore the sense of person, personal dignity and interpersonal social relatedness.

The salience of these can be seen by reflecting back upon the situation of the world in the 1930s. It was a time of great totalitarian blocks and great empires in which what mattered was the decisions not of the persons or even peoples, but of the ruling power. Step by step during the last half century there has followed the dismantling of Fascism in the 1940s, of colonialism in the 1950s and 1960s, of racism in the 1960s and 1970s, and finally in the late 1980s the dramatic collapse of Marxism as well as the emergence of women and minorities to a new equality. All this has taken place within living memory.

In retrospect one can see through all this one constant, namely, the emergence of a new sensibility to the person and in these terms a new sense of society as composed of persons acting freely. It is this positive insight which generated revulsion against suppression, mobilized the great armies and movements of independence, and finally brought the implosion of the last empire.

This positive development of the phenomenon of the emergence of the person can be seen interiorly in the mind through philosophy and in the heart through religion. Philosophically, it can be traced in this century to the roots of phenomenology in the young Husserl. He was directed by Masaryk to Bretano,[1] from whose Catholic heritage he drew the sense of intentionality as the deep interior movement of the spirit. Following this lead, Husserl creatively developed a method for what modern rationalism had rejected when it was proposed earlier by Pascal and Kierkegaard, namely, the recognition and reflective elaboration of the interior life of the person with its subjectivity and spirit. This was subsequently developed by Heidegger as a route to Being itself[2] understood as the foundational reality. This transcended all particular beings, but emerged into time in and through the interior spiritual life of the conscious human being or *dasein*.

The other facet of this interior life of the person is religion. This is lived not only with the mind but more amply with the heart as well, from which emerges the response of love and commitment of which social life is the fruit. It is then to religion as enlivening and fulfilling the new sense of the interior life of the person that we must look for insight into the reality of Islam, which quintessentially is the desire to be faithful in response to God. This is a people who truly attempt to let God be God in their lives. In this they have much to teach all who would be religious and faithful to God.

SOCIETY AND CULTURAL TRADITIONS

We have seen above the way in which a heightened sense of person was developed through the phenomenologies of Husserl who shed light on human interiority and his student Heidegger who traced this to Being, including its transcendence. This work was carried forward by Heidegger's successor H.G. Gadamer who extended the sense of interiority to the community as it lives in space and through time. This is the expression of our consciousness as it emerges or comes to life in interaction with others. This interaction begins with one's mother whose heartbeat first summons us to consciousness in the womb, it is integrated by our family and neighborhood with whom we grow, and it is extended by our language community from which we assimilate a whole approach to the world around us.

This pattern of human sensibility is not only synchronic, however. Rather it is learned and developed cumulatively through time. This is not merely a matter of sense experience, feedback mechanisms and pragmatic learning of the means to protect our bodily life. It is as well a process of discovering what is worth realizing in life. Hence, it is a process of deep discovery of human values including those of religion and of the God who is thereby honored and obeyed.

Over time this generates the content of a culture as our interior faith expresses itself in the way we live with others. It shapes our interpersonal relations including the way we dress and present ourselves to others, the respect we have for them, the way we organize our family life, business and community relations. Conversely, that we grow up in a community which is thus marked provides a way in which we can live with others in peace — and thus live fully and with human dignity.

In this way, the renewed sense of person has led to a renewed sense of community and hence of the culture of the community. This special sense of the community in Islam has extended stably through time, due especially to the Koran as the one religious source to which all its members turn in faith. But they consider also the saying and actions of the Prophet and of his first Companions, and the life of the community in Medina. They guard these as guides to the way in which the Koran and the will of God are lived.

We must always return to the sources, learn from the content and example of the past, and draw upon it in our lives. Fazlar Rahman noted that it has always been characteristic of renewals in Islamic life to return to its roots, not simply to respect the historic past, but to rediscover what is essential and salvific. This suggests the importance now of a return to the treasury of the Islamic heritage with its rich store of sacred wisdom. This has been drawn from the sources and shaped into a rich culture through the multiple circumstances of history and geography.

We must recognize, moreover, the fact and reality of change. In the past few had a higher education and there was no instant radio news and analysis. These means and the possibilities of travel have vastly extended our world. How then can the same religious inspiration of the Prophet and the community of Islam shape not only what was the life of older times, but that of the times in which we live?

Here we need to extend the cultural pattern of Islamic life as synchronic into the dimension of time. Its diachronic character must be newly appreciated so that it can live fully through time as the tempo of change increases.

The term 'tradition' can be revealing. It comes from the Latin term *tradere*, that is, to pass on. This suggests that to preserve what has been received means not merely repeating the past, but finding out how it can be lived in new circumstances. That is, enabling it to live in our times, and then passing it on as living and life-giving to the next generation.

This, of course, requires deep knowledge or insight, and a great love of the content of tradition. But it requires as well another power, that of imagination. This power stands between the body with its senses and the spirit. Being on the side of the senses it works with images or pictures, but in pointing toward the spirit it does not reject what has been seen or heard but reformulates and reorders that in new ways. In this it is like a spectroscope opening out the full range of contents and like a kaleidoscope in suggesting the many combinations in which these contents can be ordered and lived. This is the tool for creative new insight and application, making it possible to live the past creatively in our day and to pass it on to future generations.

Henri Corbin states this well adding that "freeing that past . . . is to give it a future again, to make it significant." In this work scholars must play an important, indeed, an essential, role, not only in deepening the understanding of the heritage, but in building bridges for transposing its meaning to the present and in finding here its appropriate and creative applications. By way of example, this could mean the investigation of such issues as the immanence of the divine in human history; the manner of responsible human initiative in the realization of Providence; the mode and construction of the networks needed to implement the social life of a people; and the manner in which each people can make its creative contribution to a broader world civilization which prospers in productive interchange, benevolence and peace.

Islam

To see how this is perceived and responded to by Christianity we turn to the words of the Second Vatican Council of the Roman Catholic Church. The time was the early 1960s when the new sense of the person was emerging after World War II. At that point rather than simply fighting the new in order to repeat the past, this largest religious body in the world convoked its 3000 Bishops from all parts of the globe in a most solemn three-year session. Its significance can be gauged from the simple fact that Councils are held only at points of high crises which have emerged on the average of only once in two centuries. In this Council in order to work out the implications of the new interior sense of the life of the person for religion in modern times all phases of the life of the Church were reviewed. Over 700 pages of documents were drafted, deeply discussed, amended and adopted. It was a magnificent example of the structural strength of the Church to organize and respond positively, creatively and with authority to the developments of the time. Hence, its statement on Islam can be taken as a uniquely authentic religious appreciation of the faith of a people in our times.

It begins with the statement that the Church looks upon the Moslems with esteem or appreciation of their high value. It proceeds to give the reason for this esteem, namely, that:

- they adore God who is one;
- they adore God who is living;
- they adore God who is enduring;
- they adore God who is merciful;
- they adore God who is all powerful;
- they adore God who is the maker of heaven and earth;
- they adore God who is speaker to men when they submit to His degrees, even when inscrutable after the example of our father Abraham.
- they honor Christ and Mary, his virgin mother;
- they await the day of judgment which will bring the resurrection and reward of each according to his or her due; and finally, they worship God in prayer, almsgiving and fasting.[3]

The esteem of the Council was not only notional, but practical. Thus, it is followed by a reflection on the fact of past quarrels and hostilities, which it would not be realistic to ignore. But the Council then drew itself up to its full stature to declare that: "This most Sacred Synod urges all to forget this and to strive rather for mutual understanding."

On this basis it looked forward to cooperation in safeguarding and fostering those virtues which are shared by all religions and exemplified eminently in Islam, namely, social justice, moral values, peace and freedom.

From this it can be said with the highest and broadest authority that the beliefs of Islam are shared, that Moslems are admired and appreciated for professing their beliefs and for the intensity and whole-heartedness with which they dedicate themselves thereto; and that Christians individually and corporately in living their beliefs need and wish to learn from the deep faith of Moslems.

There is a shared religious base to all cultures. This envisages all creation as participations in the unique unlimited and absolute source and goal. It entails a radical compatibility, through not homogeneity, of cultures and their religious bases.

This is important to remember, precisely because there is no lack of misunderstanding and fear. It has been said well that whatever man can do he can do badly. This is true as well of religion as a virtue and work of man. The exercising of this virtue inevitably is affected by all the human pressures from within and without, not least of which can be an ardent, if less wise or balanced, desire to serve God in one's own manner. This had led some groups, acting in good faith, to ways that seem to impose unduly upon others either in proposing their faith or even suppressing the freedom of others to expression or exercise their belief.

Vatican II devoted a whole document to this issue of religious liberty[4] as an acquisition of our times which it called upon all to recognize, protect and promote. It is important then, if a small minority of unenlightened if ardent Christians or Moslems lack adequate respect for the beliefs of others, that this not be allowed to hide the tolerance long revered by Moslems or the freedom proclaimed by Christians. Extreme minorities, precisely as extreme, do not reflect the deep truth of these two religious cultures. It is important that small minorities not cloud the issue, and that other religions not take them as expressing the authentic meaning and thrust of that culture or people.

Moreover, it can be said with the highest and broadest authority that this applies to practice as well as to principle; that the beliefs of Islam are shared by Christians; that Moslems are admired and appreciated for professing their beliefs and for the intensify and completeness with which they dedicate themselves thereto; and that Christians individually and corporately in living their beliefs need and wish to learn from the deep faith of Islam.

In view of this, how can the West and Islam in fact realize the desire expressed by Vatican II and take up common cause on behalf of all mankind in safeguarding and fostering social justice, moral values, peace and freedom?

Today, we have a new reality. In earlier centuries the meeting of our cultures was carried out on the frontiers where relations were often external and violent. There was the long combat with Byzantium, the Crusades, the wars of the Balkans. Commerce brings materials, notably oil, from afar and makes it an indispensable part of everyday life. The new technology of communications brings distant realities into our homes; the development of education makes them part of our growth and learning; the emerging sense of interiority encourages us to interiorize these exchanges in our hearts and minds. We meet inescapably in every facet of our lives. Consequently, we can cooperate and we must learn to do so. But in so doing we must not destroy what is distinctive of each and thereby impoverish all. This implies then that if we are to be present to each other we must not only learn from each other but how to integrate this new insight into our lives. In this the hope is to contribute mutually.

Islam with its rich sense of faithfulness to God based on its sense of his unity and primacy can contribute to the religious life of the West what is most essential, the sense of God.

In return, the Church in the West has struggled for many centuries with the threats that Islam most fears, namely, reductivism, rationalism and materialism. It has learned by its failures as well as its successes how to live as religious in a culture that is distracted by possessions and inundated by images. These are projected with techniques drawn from sophisticated psychological research and at the service of commercial and ideological interests often contrary to religion. It could be expected that Christianity which has grown with these challenges in the West might have insights which could be helpful in protecting and promoting religious life in Islam in these times of change.

In his book, *Seize the Moment*,[5] Richard Nixon suggests a principle for such mutual exchange, namely, that it is not our business to determine what the other will be or do, but only to help them become what they will to be. This reflects well the new sense of the person and the new respect for the interiority of the spirit and hence for human freedom. It echoes the classical sense of the love of benevolence in which the good is willed for the other without seeking what this will do for us. We have all experienced this in our families where we came first to know of God's creative benevolence in our lives.

This is the suggestion of Vatican II, namely, that we have much to share and the ability to cooperate in safeguarding and fostering social justice and moral virtues. In this manner it will be possible for religion to make a creative contribution to a broader world civilization which prospers in productive interchange, benevolence and peace.

NOTES

1. *Czech Philosophy in the XXth Century*, Novy, J. Gabriel and J. Hroch, eds. (Washington: The Council for Research in Values

and Philosophy, 1994), pp. 10-20, 110-116.

2. *Being and Time*, trans. J. Macquaraie and E. Robinson (New York: Harper and Row, 1962). See also Vensus A. George *Authentic Human Destiny: The Paths of Shankara and Heidegger* (Washington: The Council for Research in Values and Philosophy, 1998).

3. *Nostra aetate*, in *The Documents of Vatican II*, ed. A. Abbot and J. Gallagher (New York: America Press, 1966), pp. 663, n. 3.

4. *Dignities Humanae, ibid.,* pp. 675-686.

5. Richard Nixon, *Seize the Moment* (New York: Simon & Schuster, c1992).

CHAPTER VIII

SAMUEL HUNTINGTON AND THE RELIGIOUS BASIS FOR CIVILIZATION
(Cultural Research Bureau, Tehran)

The issue of faith and reason is ancient and perduing. But today it reflects the profound change in attitude and even in culture which is taking place at this transition of the millennia. The particular theme is suggested by a recent encyclical, *"Fides et Ratio,"* by Pope John Paul II in Rome. This takes an interesting strategic turn. Since the Enlightenment it has been commonly thought in academic circles that reason would solve all the human problems; faith was considered no longer necessary and was expected with time to atrophy and fade away.

In fact, it seems to be quite the contrary. The great hope placed in reason has now been strongly questioned by the postmodern philosophers who tend to be very skeptical about its powers. So much so, indeed, that there is danger that reason will be discarded entirely and supplanted by subjectivity.

In these circumstances the Encyclical says rather that we cannot do without reason, but that reason finds its great defense in faith. Faith as the received belief of peoples, elaborated on the basis of experience over the centuries. It identifies the basic character of reality as originating in an act of wisdom and love from an all wise and powerful creator, rather than in a senseless collision of matter. It presents humans as images of this wisdom and hence as having the competency not only to comprehend their physical and social universe, but to understand this in terms of the infinite wisdom and love of its transcendent source and goal.

Thus, rather than reason being all powerful and faith not being needed, the Encyclical suggests that we begin from faith — from our scriptures: the Qu'ran and the Bible — and there garner a sense of human life and destiny. To this there is need to add a strong development of philosophy working in its own proper terms. Thence, it will be possible to proceed to develop an adequate theology through cooperation of faith and reason in order to come to a more detailed and articulate understanding of the messages received long ago through the Prophets and their meaning for faithful progress in our day.

In this document then faith returns as the defender of reason to encourage those who have become discouraged with scientific reason to continue their work and to bring this to full effectiveness through cooperation with faith.

S. Huntington. This sheds light on a number of other contemporary writings. One is the work by Sammuel Huntington, now well-known throughout the world, entitled *The Clash of Civilizations and the Remaking of World Order.* He notes there that a number of modes of understanding and of developing a world order have been surpassed. There were emperors in the past, but they are no longer. There have been nation states, but increasingly they are no longer self-sufficient and need to work with other nations within such international organizations as The United Nations, The World Bank, The International Monetary Fund, etc. The idea of a nation state as a perfect society in the sense of being totally self-sufficient so that nothing else was needed seems a thing of the past. The ideologies which attempted within their single system to articulate the whole of life moved inexorably towards the Cold War extremes of the individualism of liberalism and the communalism of Marxist ideology, but now there is great pessimism not about their adequacy but about the ability of reason from which they sprang.

Today, as people look back over this century they see that it has been so violent and led to such destruction that many say we must destroy reason in order to free ourselves from this very dangerous force in the world. There is an anti-foundationalist movement to destroy all foundations, along with a general concern to remove all Absolutes, whether persons or principles.

Finding ourselves in a situation in which the previous modes of developing a world order seem to have failed, we now are forced to confront the question of what will be the new mode for developing a world order.

Huntington seeks the new modes of coming together on what gives people confidence and trust in one another. He cites these in pairs, the one is blood and the other is belief or, correspondingly, family and faith. In terms of these two elements we live, develop our horizons, elaborate our values, and have confidence in one another and in life as a whole. Consequently, the possibilities of coming together gravitate around these two elements of family relationships or blood and of faith or religion. Together they generate a culture and civilization as the way in which people understand and live their lives.

In this light he sees seven or eight major civilizations, which are characterized by a certain consanguinity and a basic belief system: Chinese, Islam, Christianity, etc. The future world promises to consist neither in a bipolar set of ideologies nor in a sequence of totally independent nation states, but rather in these civilizations in which people share understanding, concern, a belief system, and world view; these are the natural ways of coming together. Huntington judges to be mistaken rationalism's consideration of this as a return to a prerational and superstitious stage, thinking itself capable of doing the work of belief. Instead, we appear to be in a post rationalist period in which a new set of human sensibilities and an urgent and promising new agenda is emerging.

F. Fukuyama. Another figure, perhaps equally famous with Huntington, is Francis Fukuyama, who wrote *The End of History.* It sees capitalism as now a matter of common consensus so that conflict has ended and with it history in Hegel's sense of the term. But in a subsequent work entitled: *Trust, Social Virtues and the Creation of Prosperity* he carries this thought further to note that for prosperity in business there is need for trust between people. He acknowledges sets of virtues cited by Weber as keys to capitalism: diligence, saving, rationality, innovation, risk-taking, etc. But Fukuyama notes that these will not work in the economic order unless they are undergirded by a sense of honesty, reliability, cooperation and responsibility. If those are lacking and there is no trust, then initiative cannot go forward nor will it achieve its reward. This foundational set of virtues comes from the cultures, which in turn are grounded in faith.

Hence both thinkers at this turn of the millennium point towards the future saying that rationality has not been enough and will not be enough, and that there is need for an undergirding confidence and trust in culture built upon family and faith.

But will such a world proceeding on the basis of faiths, with the cultures and civilizations they generate, be one of order or of chaos, will it be peaceful or conflictual? Huntington says it will be a clash for he sees conflict as inherent in multiple identities. Indeed he foresees a mega-clash because it will be one of great populations and carried on with deep passion. For what touches one's religious beliefs touches one's identity most profoundly and evokes the strongest reactions. As a result he sees the world coordinated on the basis of civilizations as a situation of great conflict. We know too well that civilizations and beliefs can be involved in great struggles. Of course, Huntington is not promoting this, but he considers it to be inevitable future and seeks how to proceed in such a world.

In Iran one hears another view, namely, that it must be not a clash, but a dialogue of civilizations. This has been proposed as a theme to The United Nations and the world has responded positively. It is broadly realized, in other words, that we must find ways in which the relationship of civilizations, founded upon the relationship of beliefs, can be a positive dialogue. Contrary to the prediction of Marx and others, Huntington shows that religion is not atrophying and disappearing. Rather, it is so much the reality of the future that he makes it a main focus of much of his book. In so doing he raises, but does not seem to respond to the issues of how religions can be related positively.

Faith. Huntington considers that what people are concerned about is their self-identity. Others would say that self-interest is central, but he points out that one cannot speak of self-interest without having a self and knowing something about what that is. But to move from self-interest to self-identity is to touch on culture, family and faith. Hence, the search for self-identity is related by Huntington to the development and renewal of the search for faith.

He provides many different statistics to support his thesis that religion is not atrophying and disappearing as expected by the Enlightenment but showing new strength. Whereas the liberal supposition was that the more people were educated the less they would be involved in belief, it has turned out to be the opposite. This is true of Islam most of all. Where it was projected that the more people moved away from the village to the city the more they would be forgetful of their religious bonding, the opposite has proven true.

Coming to the city means becoming more anonymous and this having to rediscover and reaffirm one's identity, which is founded in one's beliefs. Similarly, where increasing education was expected to militate against faith this has proven not to be true, and for the same reason.

Further, demographics indicate that in the future the populations which are more religiously oriented and have a higher birthrate will be increasing, while those more effected by a secular rationalism will have lower birthrates and decrease. The demographics notably favor the areas strongest in belief.

Moreover, he speaks of the increasing ability of those areas which previously were more isolated now to communicate in a world of intensifying global interaction. For the last 500 years Europe was the center from which first explorers, then merchants, and later industrialists went out to other parts of the world. Now the world is very much interconnected. Hence, Huntington projects a great shift in power in which the non-European areas will become much the stronger.

Overall he sees attention to faith as strongly increasing. Conversely, he is not hopeful about the liberal formula from the time of the so-called "Peace of Westphalia" according to which religion was removed from public life. First of all this is false, for he has argued at great length that in most of the world and for most people faith will not be removed from global interchange but will play an increasingly powerful role. Second it would be immoral because to force people to attenuate their faith or to remove it from the public sphere of their lives could be carried out only by forcing people against their will — which, in turn, contradicts the liberal position on freedom. This contradiction would seem to be quite operative at the present time when for participation in the international monetary system and interaction in trade, etc., a condition has been the development of liberal system, with which many identify the meaning of democracy. In this system religion is removed from the public square where only the secular is allowed. This, Huntington notes, is not only false and immoral, but dangerous because unreal. He concludes then to the prospect of a strong religious development and a markedly religious future which will ground and fortify the self-identity of most of the civilizations.

Conflict or Cooperation. Having thus concluded that civilizations will not lose their identity and slide into a universal univocous and indistinguishable uniformity, Huntington then seems to suppose that any identities are contradictory to all other identities. This is a very strong element in so-called Western rationalist thought. As essentially analytic, it tends to break things down into their minimal components. Thus, Descartes recommended seeking the minimal natures and to develop such ideas sufficiently clearly to be able to distinguish each from all other ideas. Such clear and distinct ideas were to be had not only of each minimal nature but of the connection between them. Thus everything becomes dissociated and there results an atomic sense of individuals contradictory one to another.

Hobbes would see that these identities are not only contraries, but basically conflictual as they compete in search of their own self-interest: "Man is wolf to man" and conflict is the natural state of man. The best one can do is to attenuate this to some degree. This supposition would seem to run through the thought of Huntington. Just after his article was published in *Foreign Affairs*, Tang Yijie, the specialist in Chinese culture and founder of the International Institute of Chinese Culture in Beijing, wrote an article about the thesis of Huntington for *Science*, the review of the National Academy of Social Science, Beijing. He considered Huntington to have misunderstood civilizations as attack modes, whereas in reality they are modes of understanding and appreciation. Indeed, for China harmony is the great value: to live the Chinese civilization is not to attack Islam or some other part of the world, but to seek harmony with nature and with other peoples.

Semou Pathé Gueye, philosopher and former Parliamentarian from Dakar, has suggested that Huntington has deceived himself. He rightly establishes each culture as a paradigm and provides extensive statistical basis for this. But he then proceeds to suppose that these paradigms are incommensurable after the term of Thomas Kuhn. But this term has been found to have some 60 different usages in Kuhn's writings themselves. With no substantiation whatsoever Huntington supposes an incommensurability according to which civilizations can in no way understand each other and hence are destined to lurch toward clash and conflict.

Huntington would seem to be thinking in terms of self-interest, which he sees as contrasting and conflicting with others. This may be a characteristic of Huntington's Anglo-Saxon context, but not of the world.

Religion. Instead, if the world will be organized on the basis of broad civilizations and if these broad civilizations are founded on religions, then the real question is whether religions are in essence conflictual or relational — and under what conditions; and what religions can do about attenuating or overcoming general conditions of conflict.

Here it is important to note that there are different levels of life. One is the economic, which works in terms of profit. This is marked by a sense of competition, because material goods if had by one cannot be had by another; things consumed by one are not available to others. The world, when seen simply on a material or economic basis, is marked by principles of competition at least, if not of conflict.

Second, if one moves beyond the economic to the political level, one finds a world ordered in terms of power, control and ascendancy over others. This too is a basis for conflict. Only when one moves beyond this to the level of the spirit does one find oneself at a level which does not in principle imply conflict. When one expresses an idea one does not lose it, but shares it with others; indeed doing so helps one better understand the idea. The goods of the spirit are not used up or held by one alone, but rather are best communicated and shared.

Consequently, if religion is archetypically the level of the spirit, the attitude it generates is not in principle one of conflict, but one of openness and communication. Dialogue then between religions, and between the cultures and civilizations they found, should be a something natural. In Christianity this is reflected in the notion of the "good news" or "*evangelium*" for good news must be shared. This is the reason why the message of the prophets must be shared and why they exercise so magnetic an attraction on peoples everywhere.

An organization of the world not in terms of economics or of power, but of the spirit should not in principle be a situation of conflict, as Huntington supposes. If these civilizations are based on religion and the goods of the spirit then the prospect is one of communication and sharing. Where this is not so one must ask why it is not so, and proceed on the principle that peace and cooperation are natural and can be made to prevail.

Professor Abdullah Laroui in his *Islam et Modernité* suggests that the situation into which we are moving should help to overcome conflict. He suggests that Christianity and Islam have been too close together, with Islam defining itself by contrast to Christianity. In such a situation of tension he suggests adding more horizons so that both are in a broader context with the Chinese, Hindus, etc., in order to reduce mutual tensions. The present period of globalization makes this possible and even inevitable.

Nicholas of Cusa. A figure who developed this theme most intensively into a well-rounded philosophy is Nicholas of Cusa, a layman working for the Pope at the time when Constantinople-Istanbul changed hands between the Eastern Orthodox Christian empire and Islam. Nicholas of Cusa was sent as a Papal Legate to Istanbul. When he returned to Rome he suggested that the situation might not be as disastrous as people thought. David de Leonadis has studied Cusa's sense of unity in *Ethical Implications of Unity and the Divine in Nicholas of Cusa* (Washington: The Council for Research in Values and Philosophy, 1998) and shows it to constitute a revolution in perspectives. Generally, with Aristotle our sciences and even our philosophy begin with physical things inasmuch as these are most prominent for us as sentient beings. Cusa's perspective — like that of Shankara — begins rather in terms of the one creative source and goal of all creatures. Thinking in terms of the Almighty and its unity, creation forms a unity rather than a situation of conflict one with another.

Eugen Rice compares this to the difference between walking through a valley and seeing things serially one after another, in contrast to observing the whole valley from a hill top. Thence one can see all as in a picture that holds its many components in an integrating pattern with an overall beauty. Cusa proceeds in this fashion to note that to think in terms of the whole is to see the particular as the whole contracted. The whole is contributed to and realized in this world by the particular beings, which then are the whole in contracted form.

In this light, one is not just a speck of dust on the valley floor, but rather in a truer sense one is the whole contracted. Because of this one can no longer think of oneself without relating to others, for one's definition, meaning and significance includes that of others.

This is not a situation of individuals or civilizations in conflict. Rather, it is impossible to think of oneself or to identify with one's civilization without relating to others, for one's definition of oneself includes the relationship to others. The same is true of civilizations. Thus, reality is not a set of individuals in a situation of conflict. Rather, the basic human reality is relational: to live and to thrive is precisely to build on that relationship.

In the sense of Nicolas of Cusa what we have then is neither a clash nor even, I would say, a dialogue of civilizations, but something much closer in which we share our concerns and efforts, Cusa's vision then is not esoteric, but reflects each person's basic experience in their family as supporting their development. There one's happiness is that of the other family members and vice versa. This is the reality we live, and it is the philosophy of Nicolas of Cusa.

His vision is religious seeing all as one within the whole which reflects the divine. Moreover, it is dynamically religious being predicated upon the unity of the one source and goal of all. Hence, all are seen as being on pilgrimage from source to one goal. There are many paths, but all lead to the one God. Because the paths are convergent, the achievement of each is the achievement of all. If one can help one would be most happy to do so. It would be as much a fulfillment to help another person or civilization to proceed along their path as to help persons in my culture or religion to follow theirs. All are proceeding toward the same goal by the munificence of God by which he shares his goodness and draws all to himself.

This suggests a new way of reading and transcending the book of Huntington. With him it sees religion as a foundational organizing principle for the world. However, his supposition that the multiplicity of civilizations must be conflictual is transcended. If civilizations are in fact religiously founded and if the religions insist that there is one God, then we are not merely in a dialogue, but in a cooperative effort in which it is possible to overcome conflict and proceed through cooperation toward a shared goal.

CHAPTER IX

CONFLICT OR COOPERATION
BETWEEN CIVILIZATIONS
(Center for Dialogue among Civilizations, Tehran)

It is an honor to be invited to speak at this Center for Dialogue among Civilizations. On the one hand, I wish to congratulate President Khatami and the people of Islam for this initiative which, for reasons I will detail below, reflects their unique identity and contribution to the world. On the other hand, I note both a similarity and a contrast to the well-know work by Samuel P. Huntington, *The Clash of Civilizations and the Remaking of World Order.*

Consequently, it would seem appropriate to ask regarding this project of dialogue of civilizations and the projection by Samuel Huntington of a clash of civilizations: what is the difference between the two and what difference does it make? To wonder is the beginning of philosophy; to wonder today about this central and urgent issue is to begin to philosophize in a contemporary and responsible manner.

My response to the above questions consists of four main steps. The first is to look at the emerging state of unity with diversity in the world today. The second is to consider Samuel Huntington's thesis that civilizations as major identities of peoples are based on religion, which is not declining but rather rising in importance and influence in people's lives. Third is to note that he sees identities as contradictory and consequently civilizations as incomparable and conflictual in nature. Thus, it becomes a matter of living with and, it would seem, living by conflict. Fourth, in contrast to the thesis of an essentially conflictual nature of cultures, and especially of civilizations as based on religion, this chapter will suggest another model, namely, not a conflictual but a convergent relation of religions and civilizations.

THE PRESENT STATE: UNITY WITH DIVERSITY

It is now commonplace to note that the world has become one. This is true in a number of ways. Psychologically it became true in a special way as people first took up space exploration, landed on the moon and were able to look back at the globe as one. If Nicholas of Cusa noted the vast difference between considering things piecemeal by reason and seeing them whole by intellect, then this act constituted a special stage in human awareness. No longer is the world made up simply of many particulars; instead individuals are the world — contracted perhaps, but world nonetheless.

To this must be added, of course, the more prosaic but powerful developments in commerce of a global market, and in communications of a global system. Finally with the end of the Cold War all this has moved from a bipolar to a one world status.

At the same time there has taken place a new interior exploration taking account not only of objective reality reducing subjects to the status of objects for inspection and manipulation, but of subjectivity lived reflexively and from within. This enables a people to take direct conscious account of the exercise of creative freedom over generations, whereby the cultures and traditions have been developed.

This provides not only an awareness of one's own cultural identity, but an analogical awareness of the distinctiveness of the cultures of other peoples. In this lies the heart of the present dilemma, namely, that the very same step in self-awareness entails as well awareness of both the cultural universe in which we stand and its inherent and essential distinctiveness, and by implication then the diversity of cultures.

In view of this Huntington notes that the world is no longer ordered either by the great empires of the past or by the nation states of the Treaty of Versailles, nor by the ideological hegemonies of the bi-polar world of the cold war era. All of these have proven alternately incapable of retaining the allegiance of people and/or of providing for their welfare.

Now in contrast the platoons are tribes and ethic peoples, the regiments they compose are the nations, and the great armies are the civilizations. The major forces which have always operated and continue to do so are rather the pair of blood and belief, that is, of family and faith. Blood and family extended to ethnicities and races represent the physical lines of relationships among humankind. Belief and faith are the major belief systems according to which we interpret our lives and respond to our challenges.

RELIGION AS THE BASIS OF CIVILIZATIONS

Huntington, as noted above, sees civilizations as based on religions. In order to elaborate his thesis that the future bodes conflict between civilizations he argues at great length the present increasing importance of the role of religion in the life of peoples and of cultures today. He does this on a number of bases.

First, interest in, and the life of, religion entails a central role as the key to a person's and a people's self-identity. Attention to this religious source intensifies to the degree that self-identity is threatened, making religion more consciously needed. Huntington observes this in the more educated and the more mobile groups.

On the enlightenment model it had always been expected that such groups would be less attentive to religion. It was supposed that to the degree that they were "enlightened," understood as being possessed of a Promethean reason, their attention to religion would atrophy and disappear. Religion, as Marx remarked was but a superstructure of an outmoded system and would disappear with human development.

In fact, however, as Huntington points out, in many cultures it is precisely among the more educated and mobile that religion appears to be either increasing or holding its own at periods of young adulthood when religious practice and concern normally decline. This is true especially of the more educated groups in the Islamic world. As they enter into new cultural and intellectual worlds and there find a challenge to their self identity this propels them to new attention to the religious foundations of their identity. Correspondingly, this same group tends to be more mobile and to move from more rural to more urban contexts. As they move away from family and from the roots of their self-understanding they find themselves in greater need of more clearly re-articulating the foundations of their life and identity. As they do so they turn greater attention to religion. Consequently, precisely where religion was expected by the Enlightenment to atrophy, in fact, the contrary is happening as attention to religion increases.

Second, the process of communication has new impact on the peoples of Islamic and Eastern cultures as their access to television programming from various cultures intensifies. This, in turn, creates a new issue of self-identity and a need for a reaffirmation of the religious roots of this self-identity.

The third reason for the projection of an ascendancy of religiously based cultures is related to the overall changes in the world. Demographically peoples who are religious in their cultural roots and consequently in their civilizations are increasing. In contrast, in the West, where secularization has attenuated attention to religion one finds declining populations. The relative disproportion between those two groups is so notable that, as we move on into the next century, the difference will become determining.

Fourth, in the global pattern of power if influence follows cultural conscious then the emerging self-identity of peoples, founded religiously, promises to translate into an increasing assertion of power by Islamic and Eastern peoples.

Fifth, Huntington's thesis about the importance of the role of religion in public life conflicts with the Western liberal effort to envisage the world in a way which abstracts from the religious dimension. The classic liberal mind traces this to the religious wars, the War of the Roses and the consequent peace of Westphalia as an agreement on the need to separate religion from political life. But this was a militarily imposed solution rather than a matter of the free assessment and assent the people. The supposition of the liberal mind that its position in this regard reflects a universal and necessary truth entails the intent of imposing upon the rest of the world this Western separation and removal of religion from public life.

Huntington sees this as false, immoral and dangerous. First, it is false because religion is in fact not declining but increasing. Second, it is immoral because, in view of this increasing adhesion by peoples to religion, to impose the Western system of separation of religion from public life is alien to Islam and the East. This requires increasing applications of power, that is, of violence by the West thereby undermining its own profession of respect for freedom. Third, it is dangerous because the balance of power is shifting towards religiously concerned peoples and inevitably will lead to the defeat of the West if it makes a principal of standing against religion and isolating it from public life.

Indeed, it would seem that this effort is being felt significantly and resented in Latin America and other parts of the world. The linking of support for economic, health, ecological and other measures to democratic reform understood in the West as the separation of religion from public life imposes the liberal secularist view by myriad and pervasive financial and other means. In response Professor Kapal on whom Huntington draws notes a significant change from the middle of the 1970s in his work *The Revenge of God*. For Islam it consists of a shift of emphasis from the modernization of Islam to the Islamization of modernization, which implies as well the desecularization of the world.

In the view of his extensive and intensive study summarized above, Huntington sees the shift as being rather towards religion and that this promises to be a decisive factor in the exercise of power in the future.

THE PROBLEM OF INCOMPARABILITY OF CIVILIZATIONS

As the major message of religion is peace, Huntington's grounding of civilizations in religion of itself would seem to entail hopes for a trend toward peace as the religious sensibilities emerge. In fact his concluding rather to a clash of civilizations suggests that he has a second premise. The fact that this is largely unstated and unexamined suggests the urgency of such an examination. In fact, the second premise of Samuel Huntington is particularly disturbing; it is that identities are essentially conflictual. Here, the basic reason is the atomistic character of modern Enlightenment thought. This thought is basically analytic attempting to divide everything into its atomic components each distinct from the other. This implies that when basic units are arrived at they are by nature conflictual and contrasting in nature.

With this atomistic vision he concludes that there are seven or eight major civilizations, each constituting the basic identity for the peoples within its sphere. On the above basis he supposes them to be automatically conflictual in character; consequently, the title of his book: the clash of civilizations.

This thesis shows up in another form expressed with Thomas Kuhn in terms of the notion of paradigms as incommensurable. In this view one cannot understand the other and consequently, wittingly or unwittingly, each is on a course of conflict with the others.

As this is a key supposition in Huntington's thought a major task of philosophers in this regard is to examine this question to see whether cultural identities are conflictual in principal or whether on the contrary, precisely as cultural and as founded on religion, they are in principal convergent.

This, of course, is not only an issue of principle but of historical practice as well. But here the fact that in the past religions have conflicted does not and should not determine the future. Rather the ongoing historical development of human understanding as we enter into a global age makes it possible to mine anew in more effective, and indeed more authentic, ways the convergent potentialities of the religions which undergird the multiple civilizations.

From the combination of the two major thesis mentioned above, namely, the increase in religious awareness and sensitivities and their supposed conflictual character Huntington sees the increasing identification in terms of religion, culture, and civilizations as generating a threat of broader conflicts. These will be passionately fought precisely because more deeply grounded, not merely in economic or geographic reasons, but rather in the most basic religious self-identifications of peoples. Hence, the imposition of one culture upon another, or one family upon another, of one faith upon another cuts to the quick and generates the most impassionate reactions.

COOPERATION BETWEEN RELIGIONS
AS CONVERGENT

By way of critique it should be noted that Huntington does not seem adequately to distinguish the levels of concern. A first level of concern is the physical realm of material goods. The interchange and interrelation of these constitutes the economic order which is entered into for motives of profit. Because physical goods are mutually exclusive and such a good possessed by one is not available to the other these natively are bases for conflict. The second level of concern is political. This is a matter of the exercise of power; again its possession by one implies a subjection of the other.

Moving beyond these two levels of economics and politics, that is, of profit and power, one comes to the spiritual level of concern. Here, in contrast to the other two goods this order is not possessed exclusively by one *vis-a-vis* the other, but can be shared.

Thus, if one shares one's knowledge with the other, one does not thereby lose it; in fact, the very process of sharing this can be a process of acquiring it more firmly. This is the experience of teachers that it is in teaching that they come finally to comprehend their subject.

In view of this it is important to note that Huntington's thesis is precisely that the focus of attention is indeed shifting from the first two levels of economic and political concerns to the third level of self identity and its religious roots. In view of this dramatic changes are taking place with far reaching implications.

In the past Jean Paul Sartre carried the Enlightenment to its logical extreme in asserting that for one to be free meant freeing oneself from any Transcendent: one could not be free if there was a God. Today all of that is being reassessed as Enlightenment reason is embarrassed with the consequences it has generated and people look for a more secure and humane dimensions of rationality. This shift appears in such fora as the United Nations, which have moved from the clashes in the Security Council of the two major Cold War economic systems to the great UN conferences on environment in Rio, on family in Cairo, on women in Beijing, and most generally to the issues of culture and minorities.

Seen then in terms of this third level of values and cultures, the self-identity of cultures which generate civilizations need not be conflictual.

Beyond this there is the foundational question whether it is possible to generate an understanding of the other which will be constituted of a positive relation and concern. Is it possible to see the other not merely as not contradictory, but as positively related to my own self-understanding and self-realization so that cultures and civilizations are by nature not conflictual but complementary. This issue of whether cultures are conflictual or cooperative is the central point of great importance.

This question might be approached first in a more external fashion. Here to answer this simply in the affirmative would be too simple for the emerging cultural self-awareness entails diversity as well as unity. Hence an answer must be complex in order to be true. In this sense it is important to consider cultures and civilizations, and their religious roots, not only inasmuch as they are similar but also inasmuch as they are dissimilar.

As similar all religions are now recognized as authentic paths to the one God and hence as convergent paths to the Holy Mountain after the image of the prophet Isaiah.

But cooperation is made possible also by the very diversity between religions and civilizations. This is true externally inasmuch as each has had its own experience in pursuing its own path to God and is therefore able to make a distinctive contribution to the others in their pilgrimage. Islam, for instance, has always stressed and exemplified fidelity to the one God and all can and should learn from Islam in this. Christianity for its part has long faced the challenges of the secularizing force of modernization. Indeed secularism is sometimes referred to as a Christian heresy carried out by and for humankind alone.

Moreover, diverse religions and civilizations are able to contribute one to another if other civilizations are looked upon not simply as alien or other, but as stimulating all to look again into their own tradition in order to enable it to speak afresh the truths we need for our times.

These hermeneutic considerations make possible new attitudes in the relation between religions and civilizations, which may be the most important for practical interaction. But they remain impeded both epistemologically and psychologically.

Abdullah Lalai in his *Islam and Modernity* mentions that for too long Islam has understood itself in relation to Christianity. In this close contact the outlook tends to be one of contrast and conflict. This he believes has restricted self-understanding to a defensive position which militates against one's own cultural creativity. Consequently, he suggests that the horizon of Islam needs to be broadened to include other great religions such as Buddhism. This indeed is happening at the present time due to the process of globalization not only of the economy, but also of political and especially informational and cultural interchange. Consequently, it becomes much more feasible in these days for Islam to understand itself in relation to the broad field of world religions and thereby to feel more free to adapt and progress. In order for this to take place requires a new outlook and a new sense of being. This is a matter of epistemology and of metaphysics.

Here, the thought of Nicolas of Cusa can be suggestive Nicolas was a lay lawyer in the service of the Pope at the time when Islam occupied Constantinople. That fact was seen in the West as a great tragedy, but Nicolas of Cusa returned from a mission to Constantinople with a strange and unaccustomed message, namely, that perhaps the presence of Islam was not as bad as was being perceived and might even be good. It would carry his thought forward a bit to conclude that possibly Christianity with Islam is better than Christianity alone. But he was centrally impressed by the fact that while absolute unicity befits the Absolute, it was impoverishing for humankind. His metaphysics and epistemology hinged upon this truth more common in Islam and with great implications for social theory.

Today many factors make us newly aware of the world as a whole. This, of course, leaves the reality of the individual components, but rather than being seen in contrast and as exterior one to the other they are seen in terms of the one whole which they constitute.

In the view of Cusa predicated upon a whole, in terms of which all is seen, each individual must appear as the whole contracted. In this light the individual is not an insignificant species in a vast universe, but is rather the one who shares consciously in the reality of the whole. Each one has the importance of the whole as its exists in and as oneself: to be is to partake in the whole.

David De Leonardis attempts to express this in two principles. The first is a principle of individuality, namely, that each individual contraction imparts to each entity an inherent value which makes it indispensable to the whole. Correspondingly, the second principle is that if the contraction of being making each thing to be everything in a contracted sense.

From this notion of contraction there follows the creation of community in which all the entities are related not externally, but ontologically on the basis of their very constitution and hence internally. This relatedness is not artificial or arbitrary, but constitutional.

As a result his vision is marked by cohesion and complementarity. All are related in a manner not dissimilar to the parts of a body. That is, each depends upon the other and it is by each that the whole achieves its goal.

Further, precisely as a contraction of the whole, in order for anything to be what it is it must in a certain sense be everything which exists. In view of this the other is in no sense alien, but rather a part of one's own definition. Implicit in this is not only that each is needed as for each member of a team. Much more, by acting with others, in the service of others and for their good, one achieves one's own fulfillment. In this the analogy to a family is perhaps the most relevant.

In all of this the central concept is that of identity in terms not of contradiction, but of relation to others. In our world of economic competition this may seem too far to reach for we have been raised up on the notion of competition. But Francis Fukuyama's work on *Trust Social Virtues and the Creation of Prosperity* suggests that this notion of relatedness and cooperation is not really distant. Indeed it may be so deceptively present that it passes unnoticed but is not inactive. He shows how the economic sphere (and by implication all areas of human interaction) needs to be grounded in this deeper sense of unity. He points out how Weber and others would identify a number of virtues as important for the development of the economic order: diligence, saving, rationality, innovation and risk taking. These are all virtues of the individual and with them one might be on the third or lower level of unity in Cusa's understanding, that is, a vision simply of many individuals alongside each other and locked in serious competition or even combat.

Fukuyama, however, points out that these virtues would be simply conflictive were it not for a deeper undergirding set of virtues of a social nature: honesty, reliability, cooperation and responsibility. Beyond any sense of competition there is required a unity within which we find ourselves related to others with whom we share and to whom we are responsible.

In this light the cooperation that now is needed between civilizations appears not to be so distant or esoteric. In contrast, it is the supposition on which we live our daily life in our restricted circumstances. As we move now to global horizons this needs to be better understood in order that is applications and implications be able to thought through in our increasingly complex world. In this it is essential that religions no longer be seen as conflictual and be excluded from public life, but be enabled to play their foundational role in understanding and motivating positive relations of cooperation not only in family and community, but in cultures and civilizations.

INDEX

COUNCIL FOR RESEARCH IN
VALUES AND PHILOSOPHY
Members

THE COUNCIL FOR
RESEARCH IN VALUES AND PHILOSOPHY

PURPOSE

Today there is urgent need to attend to the nature and dignity of the person, to the quality of human life, to the purpose and goal of the physical transformation of our environment, and to the relation of all this to the development of social and political life. This, in turn, requires philosophic clarification of the base upon which freedom is exercised, that is, of the values which provide stability and guidance to one's decisions.

Such studies must be able to reach deeply into the cultures of one's nation--and of other parts of the world by which they can be strengthened and enriched--in order to uncover the roots of the dignity of persons and of the societies built upon their relations one with another. They must be able to identify the conceptual forms in terms of which modern industrial and technological developments are structured and how these impact human self-understanding. Above all, they must be able to bring these elements together in the creative understanding essential for setting our goals and determining our modes of interaction. In the present complex circumstances this is a condition for growing together with trust and justice, honest dedication and mutual concern.

The Council for Studies in Values and Philosophy (RVP) is a group of scholars who share the above concerns and are interested in the application thereto of existing capabilities in the field of philosophy and other disciplines. Its work is to identify areas in which study is needed, the intellectual resources which can be brought to bear thereupon, and the means for publication and interchange of the work from the various regions of the world. In bringing these together its goal is scientific discovery and publication which contributes to the promotion of human kind in our times.

In sum, our times present both the need and the opportunity for deeper and ever more progressive understanding of the person and of the foundations of social life. The development of such understanding is the goal of the RVP.

PROJECTS

A set of related research efforts is currently in process; some were developed initially by the RVP and others now are being carried forward by it, either solely or conjointly.

1. *Cultural Heritage and Contemporary Change: Philosophical Foundations for Social Life.* Sets of focused and mutually coordinated continuing seminars in university centers, each preparing a volume as part of an integrated philosophic search for self-understanding differentiated by continent. This work focuses upon evolving a more adequate understanding of the person in society and looks to the cultural heritage of each for the resources to respond to the challenges of its own specific contemporary transformation.

2. *Seminars on Culture and Contemporary Issues.* This series of 10 week cross-cultural and inter-disciplinary seminars is being coordina-ted by the RVP in Washington.

3. *Joint-Colloquia* with Institutes of Philosophy of the National Academies of Science, university philosophy departments, and societies, which have been underway since 1976 in Eastern Europe and, since 1987 in China, concern the person in contemporary society.

4. *Foundations of Moral Education and Character Development.* A study in values and education which unites philosophers, psychologists, social scientists and scholars in education in the elaboration of ways of enriching the moral content of education and character development. This work has been underway since 1980 especially in the Americas.

The personnel for these projects consists of established scholars willing to contribute their time and research as part of their professional commitment to life in our society. For resources to implement this work the Council, as a non-profit organization incorporated in the District of Colombia, looks to various private foundations, public programs and enterprises.

PUBLICATIONS ON CULTURAL HERITAGE AND CONTEMPORARY CHANGE

Series I.	*Culture and Values*
Series II.	*Africa*
Series IIa.	*Islam*
Series III.	*Asia*
Series IV.	*W. Europe and North America*
Series IVa.	*Central and Eastern Europe*
Series V.	*Latin America*
Series VI.	*Foundations of Moral Education*

CULTURAL HERITAGE
AND CONTEMPORARY CHANGE

VALUES AND CONTEMPORARY LIFE

Series I. Culture and Values

ISBN   1-56518-112-3   (paper).

Vol. I.11   *Ethics at the Crossroads: Vol. 1. Normative Ethics and*
Objective   Reason,
George F. McLean,
ISBN   1-56518-022-4   (paper).

Vol. I.12   *Ethics at the Crossroads: Vol. 2. Personalist Ethics and*
Human Subjectivity,
George F. McLean,
ISBN   1-56518-024-0   (paper).

Vol. I.13   *The Emancipative Theory of Jürgen Habermas and*
Metaphysics,
Robert Badillo,
ISBN   1-56518-043-7   (cloth);   ISBN   1-56518-042-9   (paper).

Vol. I.14   *The Deficient Cause of Moral Evil According to*
Thomas Aquinas,
Edward Cook,
ISBN   1-56518-070-4   paper   (paper).

Vol. I.16   *Civil Society and Social Reconstruction,*
George F. McLean,
ISBN   1-56518-086-0   (paper).

Vol. I.17   *Ways to God, Personal and Social at the Turn of Millennia*
The Iqbal Lecture, Lahore
George F. McLean
ISBN   1-56518-123-9   (paper).

Vol. I.18   *The Role of the Sublime in Kant's Moral Metaphysics*
John R. Goodreau
ISBN   1-56518-124-7   (pbk.)

Vol. I.21   *Religion and the Relation between Civilizations:*
Lectures on Cooperation between Islamic and
Christian Cultures in a Global Horizon
George F. McLean
ISBN   1-56518-152-2   (pbk.)

CULTURAL HERITAGES AND
THE FOUNDATIONS OF SOCIAL LIFE

Series II. Africa

Vol. II.1   *Person and Community: Ghanaian Philosophical*

Studies: I,
Kwasi Wiredu and Kwame Gyeke,
ISBN 1-56518-005-4 (cloth); ISBN 1-56518-004-6 (paper).

Vol. II.2   *The Foundations of Social Life:*
Ugandan Philosophical Studies: I,
A.T. Dalfovo,
ISBN 1-56518-007-0 (cloth); ISBN 1-56518-006-2 (paper).

Vol. II.3   *Identity and Change in Nigeria:*
Nigerian Philosophical Studies, I,
Theophilus Okere,
ISBN 1-56518-068-2 (paper).

Vol. II.4   *Social Reconstruction in Africa:*
Ugandan Philosophical studies, II
E. Wamala, A.R. Byaruhanga, A.T. Dalfovo,
J.K. Kigongo, S.A. Mwanahewa and G. Tusabe
ISBN 1-56518-118-2 (paper).

Series IIA. Islam

Vol. IIA.1   *Islam and the Political Order,*
Muhammad Saïd al-Ashmawy,
ISBN 1-56518-046-1 (cloth); ISBN 1-56518-047-x (paper).

Vol. IIA.3   *Philosophy in Pakistan*
Naeem Ahmad
ISBN 1-56518-108-5 (paper).

Vol. IIA.4   *The Authenticity of the Text in Hermeneutics*
Seyed Musa Dibadj
ISBN 1-56518-117-4 (paper).

Vol. IIA.5   *Interpretation and the Problem of*
the Intention of the Author: H.-G. Gadamer vs E.D. Hirsch
Burhanettin Tatar
ISBN 1-56518-121 (paper).

Vol.IAI.6   *Ways to God, Personal and Social at the Turn of Millennia*
The Iqbal Lecture, Lahore
George F. McLean
ISBN 1-56518-123-9 (paper).

Vol.IIA.10   *Christian-Islamic Preambles of Faith*
Joseph Kenny
ISBN 1-56518-138-7 (paper).

Vol.IIA.12 *Religion and the Relation between Civilizations:*
Lectures on Cooperation between Islamic and
Christian Cultures in a Global Horizon
George F. McLean
ISBN 1-56518-152-2 (pbk.)

Series III. Asia

Vol. III.1 *Man and Nature: Chinese Philosophical Studies, I,*
Tang Yi-jie, Li Zhen,
ISBN 0-8191-7412-2 (cloth); ISBN 0-8191-7413-0 (paper).

Vol. III.2 *Chinese Foundations for Moral Education and*
Character Development, Chinese Philosophical Studies, II.
Tran van Doan,
ISBN 1-56518-033-x (cloth); ISBN 1-56518-032-1 (paper).

Vol. III.3 *Confucianism, Buddhism, Taoism, Christianity and*
Chinese Culture, Chinese Philosophical Studies, III,
Tang Yijie,
ISBN 1-56518-035-6 (cloth); ISBN 1-56518-034-8 (paper).

Vol. III.4 *Morality, Metaphysics and Chinese Culture*
(Metaphysics, Culture and Morality, Vol. I)
Vincent Shen and Tran van Doan,
ISBN 1-56518-026-7 (cloth); ISBN 1-56518-027-5 (paper).

Vol. III.5 *Tradition, Harmony and Transcendence,*
George F. McLean,
ISBN 1-56518-030-5 (cloth); ISBN 1-56518-031-3 (paper).

Vol. III.6 *Psychology, Phenomenology and Chinese Philosophy:*
Chinese Philosophical Studies, VI,
Vincent Shen, Richard Knowles and Tran Van Doan,
ISBN 1-56518-044-5 (cloth); 1-56518-045-3 (paper).

Vol. III.7 *Values in Philippine Culture and Education:*
Philippine Philosophical Studies, I,
Manuel B. Dy, Jr.,
ISBN 1-56518-040-2 (cloth); 1-56518-041-2 (paper).

Vol. III.7A *The Human Person and Society: Chinese*
Philosophical Studies, VIIA,
Zhu Dasheng, Jin Xiping and George F. McLean
ISBN 1-56518-087-9 (library edition); 1-56518-088-7 (paper).

Vol. III.8 *The Filipino Mind: Philippine Philosophical Studies II,*

Leonardo N. Mercado
ISBN 1-56518-063-1 (cloth); ISBN 1-56518-064-X (paper).

Vol. III.9   *Philosophy of Science and Education:*
Chinese Philosophical Studies IX,
Vincent Shen and Tran Van Doan
ISBN 1-56518-075-5 (cloth); 1-56518-076-3 (paper).

Vol. III.10   *Chinese Cultural Traditions and Modernization:*
Chinese Philosophical Studies, X,
Wang Miaoyang, Yu Xuanmeng and George F. McLean
ISBN 1-56518-067-4 (library edition); 1-56518-068-2 (paper).

Vol. III.11   *The Humanization of Technology and Chinese Culture:*
Chinese Philosophical Studies XI,
Tomonobu Imamichi, Wang Miaoyang and Liu Fangtong
ISBN 1-56518-116-6 (paper).

Vol. III.12   *Beyond Modernization: Chinese Roots of Global*
Awareness: Chinese Philosophical Studies, XII,
Wang Miaoyang, Yu Xuanmeng and George F. McLean
ISBN 1-56518-089-5 (library edition); 1-56518-090-9 (paper).

Vol. III.13   *Philosophy and Modernization in China:*
Chinese Philosophical Studies XIII,
Liu Fangtong, Huang Songjie and George F. McLean
ISBN 1-56518-066-6 (paper).

Vol. III.14   *Economic Ethics and Chinese Culture:*
Chinese Philosophical Studies, XIV,
Yu Xuanmeng, Lu Xiaohe, Liu Fangtong,
Zhang Rulun and Georges Enderle
ISBN 1-56518-091-7 (library edition); 1-56518-092-5 (paper).

Vol. III.15   *Civil Society in a Chinese Context:*
Chinese Philosophical Studies XV,
Wang Miaoyang, Yu Xuanmeng and Manuel B. Dy
ISBN 1-56518-084-4 (paper).

Vol. III.16   *The Bases of Values in a Time of Change:*
Chinese and Western: Chinese Philosophical Studies, XVI
Kirti Bunchua, Liu Fangtong, Yu Xuanmeng, Yu Wujin
ISBN 1-56518-114-X (paper).

Vol. IIIB.1   *Authentic Human Destiny: The Paths of*
Shankara and Heidegger
Vensus A. George
ISBN 1-56518-119-0 (paper).

Series IV. Western Europe and North America

Vol. IV.1 *Italy in Transition: The Long Road from the First to
the Second Republic: The 1997 Edmund D. Pellegrino Lecture
on Contemporary Italian Politics*
Paolo Janni
ISBN 1-56518-120-4 (paper).

Vol. IV.2 Italy and The European Monetary Union: *The 1997 Edmund
D. Pellegrino Lecture on Contemporary Italian Politics*
Paolo Janni
ISBN 1-56518-128-X (paper).

Series IVA. Central and Eastern Europe

Vol. IVA.1 *The Philosophy of Person: Solidarity and Cultural
Creativity: Polish Philosophical Studies, I,*
A. Tischner, J.M. Zycinski,
ISBN 1-56518-048-8 (cloth); ISBN 1-56518-049-6 (paper).

Vol. IVA.2 *Public and Private Social Inventions in
Modern Societies: Polish   Philosophical Studies, II,*
L. Dyczewski, P. Peachey, J. Kromkowski,
ISBN 1-56518-050-x (cloth). paper ISBN 1-56518-051-8 (paper).

Vol. IVA.3 *Traditions and Present Problems of Czech Political
Culture: Czechoslovak Philosophical Studies, I,*
M. Bedná , M. Vejraka
ISBN 1-56518-056-9 (cloth); ISBN 1-56518-057-7 (paper).

Vol. IVA.4 *Czech Philosophy in the XXth Century:
Czech Philosophical Studies, II,*
Lubomír Nový and Jirí Gabriel,
ISBN 1-56518-028-3 (cloth); ISBN 1-56518-029-1 (paper).

Vol. IVA.5 *Language, Values and the Slovak Nation: Slovak
Philosophical Studies, I,*
Tibor Pichler and Jana Gašparíková,
ISBN 1-56518-036-4 (cloth); ISBN 1-56518-037-2 (paper).

Vol. IVA.6 *Morality and Public Life in a Time of Change:
Bulgarian Philosophical Studies, I,*
V. Prodanov, M. Stoyanova,
ISBN 1-56518-054-2 (cloth); ISBN 1-56518-055-0 (paper).

Luis Jolicoeur

ISBN 1-56518-104-2 (paper).

Vol. V.4 *Love as theFoundation of Moral Education and Character Development*

Luis Ugalde, Nicolas Barros, George F. McLean

ISBN 1-56518-080-1 (paper).

Vol. V.5 *Human Rights, Solidarity and Subsidiarity: Essays towards a Social Ontology*

Carlos E. A. Maldonado

ISBN 1-56518-110-7 (paper).

FOUNDATIONS OF MORAL EDUCATION AND CHARACTER DEVELOPMENT

Series VI. Foundations of Moral Education

Vol. VI.1 *Philosophical Foundations for Moral Education and Character Development: Act and Agent,*

G. McLean, F. Ellrod,

ISBN 1-56518-001-1 (cloth); ISBN 1-56518-000-3 (paper).

Vol. VI.2 *Psychological Foundations for Moral Education and Character Development: An Integrated Theory of Moral Development,*

R. Knowles,

ISBN 1-56518-003-8 (cloth); ISBN 1-56518-002-x (paper).

Vol. VI.3 *Character Development in Schools and Beyond,*

Kevin Ryan, Thomas Lickona,

ISBN 1-56518-058-5 (cloth); ISBN 1-56518-059-3 (paper).

Vol. VI.4 *The Social Context and Values: Perspectives of the Americas,*

O. Pegoraro,

ISBN 0-8191-7354-1 (cloth); ISBN 0-8191-7355-x (paper).

Vol. VI.5 *Chinese Foundations for Moral Education and Character Development,*

Tran van Doan,

ISBN 1-56518-033 (cloth), ISBN 1-56518-032-1 (paper).

The International Society for Metaphysics

Vol.1   *Person and Nature*
George F. McLean and Hugo Meynell, eds.
ISBN 0-8191-7025-9 (cloth); ISBN 0-8191-7026-7 (paper).

Vol.2   *Person and Society*
George F. McLean and Hugo Meynell, eds.
ISBN 0-8191-6924-2 (cloth); ISBN 0-8191-6925-0 (paper).

Vol.3   *Person and God*
George F. McLean and Hugo Meynell, eds.
ISBN 0-8191-6937-4 (cloth); ISBN 0-8191-6938-2 (paper).

Vol.4   *The Nature of Metaphysical Knowledge*
George F. McLean and Hugo Meynell, eds.
ISBN 0-8191-6926-9 (cloth); ISBN 0-8191-6927-7 (paper).

The series is published and distributed by: The Council for Research in Values and Philosophy, Cardinal Station, P.O. Box 261, Washington, D.C. 20064, Tel. 202/319-5636; Tel. message/Fax. 202/319-6089; e-mail: cua-rvp@cua.edul; website: http://www.philosophy.cua.edu/rvp.

Prices: -- Europe and North America: cloth $45.00; paper $17.50; plus shipping: surface, $3.50 first volume; $1.00 each additional; UPS, $5 first copy; air, $7.20. -- Latin American and Afro-Asian editions: $4.00 per volume; plus shipping: sea, $1.75; air, Latin America $5.70; Afro-Asia: $9.00.